DICTIONARY
THEME – BASED

British English Collection

ENGLISH-
ARABIC

The most useful words
To expand your lexicon and sharpen
your language skills

3000 words

Theme-based dictionary British English-Arabic - 3000 words

By Andrey Taranov

T&P Books vocabularies are intended for helping you learn, memorize and review foreign words. The dictionary is divided into themes, covering all major spheres of everyday activities, business, science, culture, etc.

The process of learning words using T&P Books' theme-based dictionaries gives you the following advantages:

- Correctly grouped source information predetermines success at subsequent stages of word memorization
- Availability of words derived from the same root allowing memorization of word units (rather than separate words)
- Small units of words facilitate the process of establishing associative links needed for consolidation of vocabulary
- Level of language knowledge can be estimated by the number of learned words

Copyright © 2022 T&P Books Publishing

All rights reserved No part of this book may be reproduced or utilized in any form or by any means, electronic or mechanical, including photocopying, recording or by information storage and retrieval system, without permission in writing from the publishers.

T&P Books Publishing
www.tpbooks.com

This book is also available in E-book formats.
Please visit www.tpbooks.com or the major online bookstores.

ARABIC THEME-BASED DICTIONARY
British English collection

T&P Books vocabularies are intended to help you learn, memorize, and review foreign words. The vocabulary contains over 3000 commonly used words arranged thematically.

- Vocabulary contains the most commonly used words
- Recommended as an addition to any language course
- Meets the needs of beginners and advanced learners of foreign languages
- Convenient for daily use, revision sessions, and self-testing activities
- Allows you to assess your vocabulary

Special features of the vocabulary

- Words are organized according to their meaning, not alphabetically
- Words are presented in three columns to facilitate the reviewing and self-testing processes
- Words in groups are divided into small blocks to facilitate the learning process
- The vocabulary offers a convenient and simple transcription of each foreign word

The vocabulary has 101 topics including:

Basic Concepts, Numbers, Colors, Months, Seasons, Units of Measurement, Clothing & Accessories, Food & Nutrition, Restaurant, Family Members, Relatives, Character, Feelings, Emotions, Diseases, City, Town, Sightseeing, Shopping, Money, House, Home, Office, Working in the Office, Import & Export, Marketing, Job Search, Sports, Education, Computer, Internet, Tools, Nature, Countries, Nationalities and more ...

TABLE OF CONTENTS

PRONUNCIATION GUIDE

T&P phonetic alphabet	Arabic example	English example
[a]	طفّى [ṭaffa]	shorter than in 'ask'
[ā]	إختار [iχtār]	calf, palm
[e]	هامبورجر [hamburger]	elm, medal
[i]	زفاف [zifāf]	shorter than in 'feet'
[ī]	أبريل [abrīl]	feet, meter
[u]	كلكتا [kalkutta]	book
[ū]	جاموس [ʒāmūs]	fuel, tuna
[b]	بداية [bidāya]	baby, book
[d]	سعادة [sa'āda]	day, doctor
[ḍ]	وضع [waḍ']	[d] pharyngeal
[ʒ]	الأرجنتين [arʒantīn]	forge, pleasure
[ð]	تذكار [tiðkār]	weather, together
[ẓ]	ظهر [ẓahar]	[z] pharyngeal
[f]	خفيف [xafīf]	face, food
[g]	جولف [gūlf]	game, gold
[h]	إتّجاه [ittiʒāh]	home, have
[ḥ]	أحبّ [aḥabb]	[h] pharyngeal
[y]	ذهبيّ [ðahabiy]	yes, New York
[k]	كرسيّ [kursiy]	clock, kiss
[l]	لمح [lamaḥ]	lace, people
[m]	مرصد [marṣad]	magic, milk
[n]	جنوب [ʒanūb]	sang, thing
[p]	كابتشينو [kaputʃīnu]	pencil, private
[q]	وثق [waθiq]	king, club
[r]	روح [rūḥ]	rice, radio
[s]	سخريّة [suχriyya]	city, boss
[ṣ]	معصم [mi'ṣam]	[s] pharyngeal
[ʃ]	عشاء ['aʃā']	machine, shark
[t]	تنّوب [tannūb]	tourist, trip
[ṭ]	خريطة [xarīṭa]	[t] pharyngeal
[θ]	ماموث [mamūθ]	month, tooth
[v]	فيتنام [vitnām]	very, river
[w]	ودّع [wadda']	vase, winter
[x]	بخيل [baχīl]	as in Scots 'loch'
[ɣ]	تغدّى [taɣadda]	between [g] and [h]
[z]	ماعز [mā'iz]	zebra, please
['] (ayn)	سبعة [sab'a]	voiced pharyngeal fricative
['] (hamza)	سأل [sa'al]	glottal stop

ABBREVIATIONS
used in the dictionary

Arabic abbreviations

du	-	plural noun (double)
f	-	feminine noun
m	-	masculine noun
pl	-	plural

English abbreviations

ab.	-	about
adj	-	adjective
adv	-	adverb
anim.	-	animate
as adj	-	attributive noun used as adjective
e.g.	-	for example
etc.	-	et cetera
fam.	-	familiar
fem.	-	feminine
form.	-	formal
inanim.	-	inanimate
masc.	-	masculine
math	-	mathematics
mil.	-	military
n	-	noun
pl	-	plural
pron.	-	pronoun
sb	-	somebody
sing.	-	singular
sth	-	something
v aux	-	auxiliary verb
vi	-	intransitive verb
vi, vt	-	intransitive, transitive verb
vt	-	transitive verb

BASIC CONCEPTS

1. Pronouns

I, me	ana	أنا
you (masc.)	anta	أنت
you (fem.)	anti	أنت
he	huwa	هو
she	hiya	هي
we	naḥnu	نحن
you (to a group)	antum	أنتم
they	hum	هم

2. Greetings. Salutations

Hello! (form.)	as salāmu 'alaykum!	السلام عليكم!
Good morning!	ṣabāḥ al xayr!	صباح الخير!
Good afternoon!	nahārak saʿīd!	نهارك سعيد!
Good evening!	masā' al xayr!	مساء الخير!
to say hello	sallam	سلّم
Hi! (hello)	salām!	سلام!
greeting (n)	salām (m)	سلام
to greet (vt)	sallam 'ala	سلّم على
How are you?	kayfa ḥāluka?	كيف حالك؟
What's new?	ma axbārak?	ما أخبارك؟
Bye-Bye! Goodbye!	ma' as salāma!	مع السلامة!
See you soon!	ilal liqā'!	إلى اللقاء!
Farewell!	ma' as salāma!	مع السلامة!
to say goodbye	wadda'	ودّع
Cheers!	bay bay!	باي باي!
Thank you! Cheers!	ʃukran!	شكرًا!
Thank you very much!	ʃukran ʒazīlan!	شكرًا جزيلًا!
My pleasure!	'afwan	عفوا
Don't mention it!	la ʃukr 'ala wāʒib	لا شكر على واجب
It was nothing	al 'afw	العفو
Excuse me! (fam.)	'an iðnak!	عن أذنك!
Excuse me! (form.)	'afwan!	عفوًا!!
to excuse (forgive)	'aðar	عذر
to apologize (vi)	i'taðar	إعتذر
My apologies	ana 'āsif	أنا آسف
I'm sorry!	la tu'āxiðni!	لا تؤاخذني!
to forgive (vt)	'afa	عفا

please (adv)	min faḍlak	من فضلك
Don't forget!	la tansa!	لا تنس!
Certainly!	ṭab'an!	طبعًا!
Of course not!	abadan!	أبدًا!
Okay! (I agree)	ittafaqna!	إتفقنا!
That's enough!	kifāya!	كفاية!

3. Questions

Who?	man?	من؟
What?	māða?	ماذا؟
Where? (at, in)	ayna?	أين؟

Where (to)?	ila ayna?	إلى أين؟
From where?	min ayna?	من أين؟
When?	mata?	متى؟

| Why? (What for?) | li māða? | لماذا؟ |
| Why? (~ are you crying?) | li māða? | لماذا؟ |

What for?	li māða?	لماذا؟
How? (in what way)	kayfa?	كيف؟
What? (What kind of ...?)	ay?	أي؟
Which?	ay?	أي؟

To whom?	li man?	لمن؟
About whom?	'amman?	عمّن؟
About what?	'amma?	عمّا؟
With whom?	ma' man?	مع من؟

| How many? How much? | kam? | كم؟ |
| Whose? | li man? | لمن؟ |

4. Prepositions

with (accompanied by)	ma'	مع
without	bi dūn	بدون
to (indicating direction)	ila	إلى
about (talking ~ ...)	'an	عن

| before (in time) | qabl | قبل |
| in front of ... | amām | أمام |

under (beneath, below)	taḥt	تحت
above (over)	fawq	فوق
on (atop)	'ala	على

| from (off, out of) | min | من |
| of (made from) | min | من |

| in (e.g. ~ ten minutes) | ba'd | بعد |
| over (across the top of) | 'abr | عبر |

5. Function words. Adverbs. Part 1

Where? (at, in)	ayna?	أين؟
here (adv)	huna	هنا
there (adv)	hunāk	هناك
somewhere (to be)	fi makānin ma	في مكان ما
nowhere (not in any place)	la fi ay makān	لا في أي مكان
by (near, beside)	bi ʒānib	بجانب
by the window	bi ʒānib aʃ ʃubbāk	بجانب الشبّاك
Where (to)?	ila ayna?	إلى أين؟
here (e.g. come ~!)	huna	هنا
there (e.g. to go ~)	hunāk	هناك
from here (adv)	min huna	من هنا
from there (adv)	min hunāk	من هناك
close (adv)	qarīban	قريبًا
far (adv)	baʕīdan	بعيدًا
near (e.g. ~ Paris)	ʕind	عند
nearby (adv)	qarīban	قريبًا
not far (adv)	ɣayr baʕīd	غير بعيد
left (adj)	al yasār	اليسار
on the left	ʕalaʃ ʃimāl	على الشمال
to the left	ilaʃ ʃimāl	إلى الشمال
right (adj)	al yamīn	اليمين
on the right	ʕalal yamīn	على اليمين
to the right	llal yamīn	إلى اليمين
in front (adv)	min al amām	من الأمام
front (as adj)	amāmiy	أماميّ
ahead (the kids ran ~)	ilal amām	إلى الأمام
behind (adv)	warāʼ	وراء
from behind	min al warāʼ	من الوراء
back (towards the rear)	ilal warāʼ	إلى الوراء
middle	wasaṭ (m)	وسط
in the middle	fil wasat	في الوسط
at the side	bi ʒānib	بجانب
everywhere (adv)	fi kull makān	في كل مكان
around (in all directions)	ḥawl	حول
from inside	min ad dāχil	من الداخل
somewhere (to go)	ila ayy makān	إلى أيّ مكان
straight (directly)	bi aqṣar ṭarīq	بأقصر طريق
back (e.g. come ~)	ʔīyāban	إيابًا
from anywhere	min ayy makān	من أي مكان
from somewhere	min makānin ma	من مكان ما

firstly (adv)	awwalan	أوّلًا
secondly (adv)	θāniyan	ثانيًا
thirdly (adv)	θāliθan	ثالثًا

suddenly (adv)	faʒ'a	فجأة
at first (in the beginning)	fil bidāya	في البداية
for the first time	li 'awwal marra	لأوّل مرّة
long before ...	qabl ... bi mudda ṭawīla	قبل...بمدّة طويلة
anew (over again)	min ʒadīd	من جديد
for good (adv)	ilal abad	إلى الأبد

never (adv)	abadan	أبدًا
again (adv)	min ʒadīd	من جديد
now (at present)	al 'ān	الآن
often (adv)	kaθīran	كثيرًا
then (adv)	fi ðalika al waqt	في ذلك الوقت
urgently (quickly)	'āʒilan	عاجلًا
usually (adv)	kal 'āda	كالعادة

by the way, ...	'ala fikra ...	على فكرة...
possibly	min al mumkin	من الممكن
probably (adv)	la'alla	لعلّ
maybe (adv)	min al mumkin	من الممكن
besides ...	bil iḍāfa ila ðalik ...	بالإضافة إلى...
that's why ...	li ðalik	لذلك
in spite of ...	bir raɣm min ...	بالرغم من...
thanks to ...	bi faḍl ...	بفضل...

what (pron.)	allaði	الذي
that (conj.)	anna	أنّ
something	ʃay' (m)	شيء
anything (something)	ʃay' (m)	شيء
nothing	la ʃay'	لا شيء

who (pron.)	allaði	الذي
someone	aḥad	أحد
somebody	aḥad	أحد

nobody	la aḥad	لا أحد
nowhere (a voyage to ~)	la ila ay makān	لا إلى أي مكان
nobody's	la yaxuṣṣ aḥad	لا يخص أحدًا
somebody's	li aḥad	لأحد

so (I'm ~ glad)	hakaða	هكذا
also (as well)	kaðalika	كذلك
too (as well)	ayḍan	أيضًا

6. Function words. Adverbs. Part 2

Why?	li māða?	لماذا؟
for some reason	li sababin ma	لسبب ما
because ...	li'anna ...	لأن...
for some purpose	li amr mā	لأمر ما
and	wa	و

or	aw	أو
but	lakin	لكن
for (e.g. ~ me)	li	لـ

too (excessively)	kaθīran ʒiddan	كثير جداً
only (exclusively)	faqaṭ	فقط
exactly (adv)	biḍ ḍabṭ	بالضبط
about (more or less)	naḥw	نحو

approximately (adv)	taqrīban	تقريباً
approximate (adj)	taqrībiy	تقريبي
almost (adv)	taqrīban	تقريباً
the rest	al bāqi (m)	الباقي

each (adj)	kull	كلّ
any (no matter which)	ayy	أيّ
many, much (a lot of)	kaθīr	كثير
many people	kaθīr min an nās	كثير من الناس
all (everyone)	kull an nās	كل الناس

in return for ...	muqābil ...	مقابل...
in exchange (adv)	muqābil	مقابل
by hand (made)	bil yad	باليد
hardly (negative opinion)	hayhāt	هيهات

probably (adv)	la'alla	لعلّ
on purpose (intentionally)	qaṣdan	قصدا
by accident (adv)	ṣudfa	صدفة

very (adv)	ʒiddan	جداً
for example (adv)	maθalan	مثلاً
between	bayn	بين
among	bayn	بين
so much (such a lot)	haðihi al kammiyya	هذه الكمية
especially (adv)	χāṣṣa	خاصّة

NUMBERS. MISCELLANEOUS

7. Cardinal numbers. Part 1

0 zero	ṣifr	صفر
1 one	wāḥid	واحد
1 one (fem.)	wāḥida	واحدة
2 two	iθnān	إثنان
3 three	θalāθa	ثلاثة
4 four	arba'a	أربعة
5 five	χamsa	خمسة
6 six	sitta	ستّة
7 seven	sab'a	سبعة
8 eight	θamāniya	ثمانية
9 nine	tis'a	تسعة
10 ten	'aʃara	عشرة
11 eleven	aḥad 'aʃar	أحد عشر
12 twelve	iθnā 'aʃar	إثنا عشر
13 thirteen	θalāθat 'aʃar	ثلاثة عشر
14 fourteen	arba'at 'aʃar	أربعة عشر
15 fifteen	χamsat 'aʃar	خمسة عشر
16 sixteen	sittat 'aʃar	ستّة عشر
17 seventeen	sab'at 'aʃar	سبعة عشر
18 eighteen	θamāniyat 'aʃar	ثمانية عشر
19 nineteen	tis'at 'aʃar	تسعة عشر
20 twenty	'iʃrūn	عشرون
21 twenty-one	wāḥid wa 'iʃrūn	واحد وعشرون
22 twenty-two	iθnān wa 'iʃrūn	إثنان وعشرون
23 twenty-three	θalāθa wa 'iʃrūn	ثلاثة وعشرون
30 thirty	θalāθīn	ثلاثون
31 thirty-one	wāḥid wa θalāθūn	واحد وثلاثون
32 thirty-two	iθnān wa θalāθūn	إثنان وثلاثون
33 thirty-three	θalāθa wa θalāθūn	ثلاثة وثلاثون
40 forty	arba'ūn	أربعون
41 forty-one	wāḥid wa arba'ūn	واحد وأربعون
42 forty-two	iθnān wa arba'ūn	إثنان وأربعون
43 forty-three	θalāθa wa arba'ūn	ثلاثة وأربعون
50 fifty	χamsūn	خمسون
51 fifty-one	wāḥid wa χamsūn	واحد وخمسون
52 fifty-two	iθnān wa χamsūn	إثنان وخمسون
53 fifty-three	θalāθa wa χamsūn	ثلاثة وخمسون
60 sixty	sittūn	ستّون
61 sixty-one	wāḥid wa sittūn	واحد وستّون

| 62 sixty-two | iθnān wa sittūn | إثنان وستّون |
| 63 sixty-three | θalāθa wa sittūn | ثلاثة وستّون |

70 seventy	sab'ūn	سبعون
71 seventy-one	wāḥid wa sab'ūn	واحد وسبعون
72 seventy-two	iθnān wa sab'ūn	إثنان وسبعون
73 seventy-three	θalāθa wa sab'ūn	ثلاثة وسبعون

80 eighty	θamānūn	ثمانون
81 eighty-one	wāḥid wa θamānūn	واحد وثمانون
82 eighty-two	iθnān wa θamānūn	إثنان وثمانون
83 eighty-three	θalāθa wa θamānūn	ثلاثة وثمانون

90 ninety	tis'ūn	تسعون
91 ninety-one	wāḥid wa tis'ūn	واحد وتسعون
92 ninety-two	iθnān wa tis'ūn	إثنان وتسعون
93 ninety-three	θalāθa wa tis'ūn	ثلاثة وتسعون

8. Cardinal numbers. Part 2

100 one hundred	mi'a	مائة
200 two hundred	mi'atān	مائتان
300 three hundred	θalāθumi'a	ثلاثمائة
400 four hundred	rub'umi'a	أربعمائة
500 five hundred	xamsumi'a	خمسمائة

600 six hundred	sittumi'a	ستّمائة
700 seven hundred	sab'umi'a	سبعمائة
800 eight hundred	θamānimi'a	ثمانمائة
900 nine hundred	tis'umi'a	تسعمائة

1000 one thousand	alf	ألف
2000 two thousand	alfān	ألفان
3000 three thousand	θalāθat 'ālāf	ثلاثة آلاف
10000 ten thousand	'aʃarat 'ālāf	عشرة آلاف
one hundred thousand	mi'at alf	مائة ألف
million	milyūn (m)	مليون
billion	milyār (m)	مليار

9. Ordinal numbers

first (adj)	awwal	أوّل
second (adj)	θāni	ثان
third (adj)	θāliθ	ثالث
fourth (adj)	rābi'	رابع
fifth (adj)	xāmis	خامس

sixth (adj)	sādis	سادس
seventh (adj)	sābi'	سابع
eighth (adj)	θāmin	ثامن
ninth (adj)	tāsi'	تاسع
tenth (adj)	'āʃir	عاشر

COLORS. UNITS OF MEASUREMENT

10. Colours

colour	lawn (m)	لون
shade (tint)	daraӡat al lawn (m)	درجة اللون
hue	ṣabɣit lūn (f)	لون
rainbow	qaws quzaḥ (m)	قوس قزح
white (adj)	abyaḍ	أبيض
black (adj)	aswad	أسود
grey (adj)	ramādiy	رمادي
green (adj)	aҳḍar	أخضر
yellow (adj)	aṣfar	أصفر
red (adj)	aḥmar	أحمر
blue (adj)	azraq	أزرق
light blue (adj)	azraq fātiḥ	أزرق فاتح
pink (adj)	wardiy	وردي
orange (adj)	burtuqāliy	برتقالي
violet (adj)	banafsaӡiy	بنفسجي
brown (adj)	bunniy	بني
golden (adj)	ðahabiy	ذهبي
silvery (adj)	fiḍḍiy	فضي
beige (adj)	bɛ:ӡ	بيج
cream (adj)	'āӡiy	عاجي
turquoise (adj)	fayrūziy	فيروزي
cherry red (adj)	karaziy	كرزي
lilac (adj)	laylakiy	ليلكي
crimson (adj)	qirmiziy	قرمزي
light (adj)	fātiḥ	فاتح
dark (adj)	ɣāmiq	غامق
bright, vivid (adj)	zāhi	زاه
coloured (pencils)	mulawwan	ملون
colour (e.g. ~ film)	mulawwan	ملون
black-and-white (adj)	abyaḍ wa aswad	أبيض وأسود
plain (one-coloured)	waḥīd al lawn, sāda	وحيد اللون، سادة
multicoloured (adj)	muta'addid al alwān	متعدد الألوان

11. Units of measurement

weight	wazn (m)	وزن
length	ṭūl (m)	طول

width	'ard (m)	عرض
height	irtifā' (m)	إرتفاع
depth	'umq (m)	عمق
volume	ḥaʒm (m)	حجم
area	misāḥa (f)	مساحة

gram	grām (m)	جرام
milligram	milliɣrām (m)	مليغرام
kilogram	kiluɣrām (m)	كيلوغرام
ton	ṭunn (m)	طنّ
pound	raṭl (m)	رطل
ounce	ūnṣa (f)	أونصة

metre	mitr (m)	متر
millimetre	millimitr (m)	مليمتر
centimetre	santimitr (m)	سنتيمتر
kilometre	kilumitr (m)	كيلومتر
mile	mīl (m)	ميل

inch	būṣa (f)	بوصة
foot	qadam (f)	قدم
yard	yārda (f)	ياردة

square metre	mitr murabba' (m)	متر مربّع
hectare	hiktār (m)	هكتار

litre	litr (m)	لتر
degree	daraʒa (f)	درجة
volt	vūlt (m)	فولت
ampere	ambīr (m)	أمبير
horsepower	ḥiṣān (m)	حصان

quantity	kammiyya (f)	كمّيّة
a little bit of ...	qalīl ...	قليل...
half	niṣf (m)	نصف
dozen	iθnā 'aʃar (f)	إثنا عشر
piece (item)	waḥda (f)	وحدة

size	ḥaʒm (m)	حجم
scale (map ~)	miqyās (m)	مقياس

minimal (adj)	al adna	الأدنى
the smallest (adj)	al aṣɣar	الأصغر
medium (adj)	mutawassiṭ	متوسّط
maximal (adj)	al aqṣa	الأقصى
the largest (adj)	al akbar	الأكبر

12. Containers

canning jar (glass ~)	barṭamān (m)	برطمان
tin, can	tanaka (f)	تنكة
bucket	ʒardal (m)	جردل
barrel	barmīl (m)	برميل
wash basin (e.g., plastic ~)	ḥawḍ lil ɣasīl (m)	حوض للغسيل

tank (100L water ~)	xazzān (m)	خزّان
hip flask	zamzamiyya (f)	زمزميّة
jerrycan	ʒirikan (m)	جركن
tank (e.g., tank car)	xazzān (m)	خزّان

mug	māgg (m)	ماج
cup (of coffee, etc.)	finʒān (m)	فنجان
saucer	ṭabaq finʒān (m)	طبق فنجان
glass (tumbler)	kubbāya (f)	كبّاية
wine glass	ka's (f)	كأس
stock pot (soup pot)	kassirūlla (f)	كاسرولة

| bottle (~ of wine) | zuʒāʒa (f) | زجاجة |
| neck (of the bottle, etc.) | 'unq (m) | عنق |

carafe (decanter)	dawraq zuʒāʒiy (m)	دورق زجاجيّ
pitcher	ibrīq (m)	إبريق
vessel (container)	inā' (m)	إناء
pot (crock, stoneware ~)	aṣīṣ (m)	أصيص
vase	vāza (f)	فازة

flacon, bottle (perfume ~)	zuʒāʒa (f)	زجاجة
vial, small bottle	zuʒāʒa (f)	زجاجة
tube (of toothpaste)	umbūba (f)	أنبوبة

sack (bag)	kīs (m)	كيس
bag (paper ~, plastic ~)	kīs (m)	كيس
packet (of cigarettes, etc.)	'ulba (f)	علبة

box (e.g. shoebox)	'ulba (f)	علبة
crate	ṣundū' (m)	صندوق
basket	salla (f)	سلّة

MAIN VERBS

13. The most important verbs. Part 1

to advise (vt)	naṣaḥ	نصح
to agree (say yes)	ittafaq	إتّفق
to answer (vi, vt)	aʒāb	أجاب
to apologize (vi)	iʿtaðar	إعتذر
to arrive (vi)	waṣal	وصل
to ask (~ oneself)	saʾal	سأل
to ask (~ sb to do sth)	ṭalab	طلب
to be (vi)	kān	كان
to be afraid	χāf	خاف
to be hungry	arād an yaʾkul	أراد أن يأكل
to be interested in ...	ihtamm	إهتمّ
to be needed	kān maṭlūb	كان مطلوبا
to be surprised	indahaʃ	إندهش
to be thirsty	arād an yaʃrab	أراد أن يشرب
to begin (vt)	badaʾ	بدأ
to belong to ...	χaṣṣ	خصّ
to boast (vi)	tabāha	تباهى
to break (split into pieces)	kasar	كسر
to call (~ for help)	istaɣāθ	إستغاث
can (v aux)	istaṭāʿ	إستطاع
to catch (vt)	amsak	أمسك
to change (vt)	ɣayyar	غيّر
to choose (select)	iχtār	إختار
to come down (the stairs)	nazil	نزل
to compare (vt)	qāran	قارن
to complain (vi, vt)	ʃaka	شكا
to confuse (mix up)	iχtalaṭ	إختلط
to continue (vt)	istamarr	إستمرّ
to control (vt)	taḥakkam	تحكّم
to cook (dinner)	ḥaḍḍar	حضّر
to cost (vt)	kallaf	كلّف
to count (add up)	ʿadd	عدّ
to count on ...	iʿtamad ʿala ...	إعتمد على...
to create (vt)	χalaq	خلق
to cry (weep)	baka	بكى

14. The most important verbs. Part 2

to deceive (vi, vt)	χadaʿ	خدع
to decorate (tree, street)	zayyan	زيّن

to defend (a country, etc.)	dāfaʿ	دافع
to demand (request firmly)	ṭālib	طالب
to dig (vt)	ḥafar	حفر

to discuss (vt)	nāqaʃ	ناقش
to do (vt)	ʿamal	عمل
to doubt (have doubts)	ʃakk fi	شكَ في
to drop (let fall)	awqaʿ	أوقع
to enter (room, house, etc.)	daχal	دخل

to exist (vi)	kān mawʒūd	كان موجودًا
to expect (foresee)	tanabbaʾ	تنبأ
to explain (vt)	ʃaraḥ	شرح
to fall (vi)	saqaṭ	سقط

to fancy (vt)	aʿʒab	أعجب
to find (vt)	waʒad	وجد
to finish (vt)	atamm	أتمّ
to fly (vi)	ṭār	طار
to follow ... (come after)	tabaʿ	تبع

to forget (vi, vt)	nasiy	نسي
to forgive (vt)	ʿafa	عفا
to give (vt)	aʿṭa	أعطى
to give a hint	aʿṭa talmīḥ	أعطى تلميحًا
to go (on foot)	maʃa	مشى

to go for a swim	sabaḥ	سبح
to go out (for dinner, etc.)	χaraʒ	خرج
to guess (the answer)	χamman	خمّن

to have (vt)	malak	ملك
to have breakfast	afṭar	أفطر
to have dinner	taʿaʃʃa	تعشّى
to have lunch	taɣadda	تغدّى
to hear (vt)	samiʿ	سمع

to help (vt)	sāʿad	ساعد
to hide (vt)	χabaʾ	خبأ
to hope (vi, vt)	tamanna	تمنّى
to hunt (vi, vt)	iṣṭād	إصطاد
to hurry (vi)	istaʿʒal	إستعجل

15. The most important verbs. Part 3

to inform (vt)	aχbar	أخبر
to insist (vi, vt)	aṣarr	أصرّ
to insult (vt)	ahān	أهان
to invite (vt)	daʿa	دعا
to joke (vi)	mazaḥ	مزح

to keep (vt)	ḥafaẓ	حفظ
to keep silent, to hush	sakat	سكت
to kill (vt)	qatal	قتل

to know (sb)	'araf	عرف
to know (sth)	'araf	عرف
to laugh (vi)	ḍaḥik	ضحك
to liberate (city, etc.)	ḥarrar	حرّر
to look for ... (search)	baḥaθ	بحث
to love (sb)	aḥabb	أحبّ
to make a mistake	axṭa'	أخطأ
to manage, to run	adār	أدار
to mean (signify)	'ana	عنى
to mention (talk about)	ðakar	ذكر
to miss (school, etc.)	ɣāb	غاب
to notice (see)	lāḥaẓ	لاحظ
to object (vi, vt)	i'taraḍ	إعترض
to observe (see)	rāqab	راقب
to open (vt)	fataḥ	فتح
to order (meal, etc.)	ṭalab	طلب
to order (mil.)	amar	أمر
to own (possess)	malak	ملك
to participate (vi)	iʃtarak	إشترك
to pay (vi, vt)	dafa'	دفع
to permit (vt)	raxxaṣ	رخّص
to plan (vt)	xaṭṭaṭ	خطط
to play (children)	la'ib	لعب
to pray (vi, vt)	ṣalla	صلّى
to prefer (vt)	faḍḍal	فضّل
to promise (vt)	wa'ad	وعد
to pronounce (vt)	naṭaq	نطق
to propose (vt)	iqtaraḥ	إقترح
to punish (vt)	'āqab	عاقب

16. The most important verbs. Part 4

to read (vi, vt)	qara'	قرأ
to recommend (vt)	naṣaḥ	نصح
to refuse (vi, vt)	rafaḍ	رفض
to regret (be sorry)	nadim	ندم
to rent (sth from sb)	ista'ʒar	إستأجر
to repeat (say again)	karrar	كرّر
to reserve, to book	ḥaʒaz	حجز
to run (vi)	ʒara	جرى
to save (rescue)	anqað	أنقذ
to say (~ thank you)	qāl	قال
to scold (vt)	wabbax	وبّخ
to see (vt)	ra'a	رأى
to sell (vt)	bā'	باع
to send (vt)	arsal	أرسل
to shoot (vi)	aṭlaq an nār	أطلق النار

to shout (vi)	ṣaraχ	صرخ
to show (vt)	ʿaraḍ	عرض
to sign (document)	waqqaʿ	وقّع
to sit down (vi)	ʒalas	جلس
to smile (vi)	ibtasam	إبتسم
to speak (vi, vt)	takallam	تكلّم
to steal (money, etc.)	saraq	سرق
to stop (for pause, etc.)	waqaf	وقف
to stop (please ~ calling me)	tawaqqaf	توقّف
to study (vt)	daras	درس
to swim (vi)	sabaḥ	سبح
to take (vt)	aχað	أخذ
to think (vi, vt)	ẓann	ظنّ
to threaten (vt)	haddad	هدّد
to touch (with hands)	lamas	لمس
to translate (vt)	tarʒam	ترجم
to trust (vt)	waθiq	وثق
to try (attempt)	ḥāwal	حاول
to turn (e.g., ~ left)	inʿaṭaf	إنعطف
to underestimate (vt)	istaχaff	إستخفّ
to understand (vt)	fahim	فهم
to unite (vt)	waḥḥad	وحّد
to wait (vt)	intaẓar	إنتظر
to want (wish, desire)	arād	أراد
to warn (vt)	ḥaððar	حذّر
to work (vi)	ʿamal	عمل
to write (vt)	katab	كتب
to write down	katab	كتب

TIME. CALENDAR

17. Weekdays

Monday	yawm al iθnayn (m)	يوم الإثنين
Tuesday	yawm aθ θulāθā' (m)	يوم الثلاثاء
Wednesday	yawm al arbi'ā' (m)	يوم الأربعاء
Thursday	yawm al χamīs (m)	يوم الخميس
Friday	yawm al ʒum'a (m)	يوم الجمعة
Saturday	yawm as sabt (m)	يوم السبت
Sunday	yawm al aḥad (m)	يوم الأحد
today (adv)	al yawm	اليوم
tomorrow (adv)	ɣadan	غدًا
the day after tomorrow	ba'd ɣad	بعد غد
yesterday (adv)	ams	أمس
the day before yesterday	awwal ams	أوّل أمس
day	yawm (m)	يوم
working day	yawm 'amal (m)	يوم عمل
public holiday	yawm al 'uṭla ar rasmiyya (m)	يوم العطلة الرسمية
day off	yawm 'uṭla (m)	يوم عطلة
weekend	ayyām al 'uṭla (pl)	أيام العطلة
all day long	ṭūl al yawm	طول اليوم
the next day (adv)	fil yawm at tāli	في اليوم التالي
two days ago	min yawmayn	قبل يومين
the day before	fil yawm as sābiq	في اليوم السابق
daily (adj)	yawmiy	يومي
every day (adv)	yawmiyyan	يوميًا
week	usbū' (m)	أسبوع
last week (adv)	fil isbū' al māḍi	في الأسبوع الماضي
next week (adv)	fil isbū' al qādim	في الأسبوع القادم
weekly (adj)	usbū'iy	أسبوعي
every week (adv)	usbū'iyyan	أسبوعيًا
twice a week	marratayn fil usbū'	مرّتين في الأسبوع
every Tuesday	kull yawm aθ θulaθā'	كل يوم الثلاثاء

18. Hours. Day and night

morning	ṣabāḥ (m)	صباح
in the morning	fiṣ ṣabāḥ	في الصباح
noon, midday	ẓuhr (m)	ظهر
in the afternoon	ba'd aẓ ẓuhr	بعد الظهر
evening	masā' (m)	مساء
in the evening	fil masā'	في المساء

night	layl (m)	ليل
at night	bil layl	بالليل
midnight	muntaṣif al layl (m)	منتصف الليل

second	θāniya (f)	ثانية
minute	daqīqa (f)	دقيقة
hour	sā'a (f)	ساعة
half an hour	niṣf sā'a (m)	نصف ساعة
a quarter-hour	rub' sā'a (f)	ربع ساعة
fifteen minutes	xamsat 'aʃar daqīqa	خمس عشرة دقيقة
24 hours	yawm kāmil (m)	يوم كامل

sunrise	ʃurūq aʃ ʃams (m)	شروق الشمس
dawn	faʒr (m)	فجر
early morning	ṣabāḥ bākir (m)	صباح باكر
sunset	ɣurūb aʃ ʃams (m)	غروب الشمس

early in the morning	fis ṣabāḥ al bākir	في الصباح الباكر
this morning	al yawm fiṣ ṣabāḥ	اليوم في الصباح
tomorrow morning	ɣadan fiṣ ṣabāḥ	غدًا في الصباح

this afternoon	al yawm ba'd aẓ ẓuhr	اليوم بعد الظهر
in the afternoon	ba'd aẓ ẓuhr	بعد الظهر
tomorrow afternoon	ɣadan ba'd aẓ ẓuhr	غدًا بعد الظهر

| tonight (this evening) | al yawm fil masā' | اليوم في المساء |
| tomorrow night | ɣadan fil masā' | غدًا في المساء |

at 3 o'clock sharp	fis sā'a aθ θāliθa tamāman	في الساعة الثالثة تماما
about 4 o'clock	fis sā'a ar rābi'a taqrīban	في الساعة الرابعة تقريبا
by 12 o'clock	ḥattas sā'a aθ θāniya 'aʃara	حتى الساعة الثانية عشرة
in 20 minutes	ba'd 'iʃrīn daqīqa	بعد عشرين دقيقة
in an hour	ba'd sā'a	بعد ساعة
on time (adv)	fi maw'idih	في موعده

a quarter to ...	illa rub'	إلا ربع
within an hour	ṭiwāl sā'a	طوال الساعة
every 15 minutes	kull rub' sā'a	كل ربع ساعة
round the clock	layl nahār	ليل نهار

19. Months. Seasons

January	yanāyir (m)	يناير
February	fibrāyir (m)	فبراير
March	māris (m)	مارس
April	abrīl (m)	أبريل
May	māyu (m)	مايو
June	yūnyu (m)	يونيو

July	yūlyu (m)	يوليو
August	aɣusṭus (m)	أغسطس
September	sibtambar (m)	سبتمبر
October	uktūbir (m)	أكتوبر
November	nuvimbar (m)	نوفمبر

December	disimbar (m)	ديسمبر
spring	rabī` (m)	ربيع
in spring	fir rabī`	في الربيع
spring (as adj)	rabī`iy	ربيعي
summer	ṣayf (m)	صيف
in summer	fiṣ ṣayf	في الصيف
summer (as adj)	ṣayfiy	صيفي
autumn	χarīf (m)	خريف
in autumn	fil χarīf	في الخريف
autumn (as adj)	χarīfiy	خريفيَ
winter	ʃitā' (m)	شتاء
in winter	fiʃ ʃitā'	في الشتاء
winter (as adj)	ʃitawiy	شتويَ
month	ʃahr (m)	شهر
this month	fi haða aʃ ʃahr	في هذا الشهر
next month	fiʃ ʃahr al qādim	في الشهر القادم
last month	fiʃ ʃahr al māḍi	في الشهر الماضي
a month ago	qabl ʃahr	قبل شهر
in a month (a month later)	ba'd ʃahr	بعد شهر
in 2 months (2 months later)	ba'd ʃahrayn	بعد شهرين
the whole month	ṭūl aʃ ʃahr	طول الشهر
all month long	ʃahr kāmil	شهر كامل
monthly (~ magazine)	ʃahriy	شهريَ
monthly (adv)	kull ʃahr	كل شهر
every month	kull ʃahr	كل شهر
twice a month	marratayn fiʃ ʃahr	مرّتين في الشهر
year	sana (f)	سنة
this year	fi haðihi as sana	في هذه السنة
next year	fis sana al qādima	في السنة القادمة
last year	fis sana al māḍiya	في السنة الماضية
a year ago	qabla sana	قبل سنة
in a year	ba'd sana	بعد سنة
in two years	ba'd sanatayn	بعد سنتين
the whole year	ṭūl as sana	طول السنة
all year long	sana kāmila	سنة كاملة
every year	kull sana	كل سنة
annual (adj)	sanawiy	سنويَ
annually (adv)	kull sana	كل سنة
4 times a year	arba' marrāt fis sana	أربع مرّات في السنة
date (e.g. today's ~)	tarīχ (m)	تاريخ
date (e.g. ~ of birth)	tarīχ (m)	تاريخ
calendar	taqwīm (m)	تقويم
half a year	niṣf sana (m)	نصف سنة
six months	niṣf sana (m)	نصف سنة
season (summer, etc.)	faṣl (m)	فصل
century	qarn (m)	قرن

TRAVEL. HOTEL

20. Trip. Travel

tourism, travel	siyāḥa (f)	سياحة
tourist	sā'iḥ (m)	سائح
trip, voyage	riḥla (f)	رحلة
adventure	muɣāmara (f)	مغامرة
trip, journey	riḥla (f)	رحلة
holiday	'uṭla (f)	عطلة
to be on holiday	'indahu 'uṭla	عنده عطلة
rest	istirāḥa (f)	إستراحة
train	qiṭār (m)	قطار
by train	bil qiṭār	بالقطار
aeroplane	ṭā'ira (f)	طائرة
by aeroplane	biṭ ṭā'ira	بالطائرة
by car	bis sayyāra	بالسيّارة
by ship	bis safīna	بالسفينة
luggage	aʃ ʃunaṭ (pl)	الشنط
suitcase	ḥaqībat safar (f)	حقيبة سفر
luggage trolley	'arabat ʃunaṭ (f)	عربة شنط
passport	ʒawāz as safar (m)	جواز السفر
visa	ta'ʃīra (f)	تأشيرة
ticket	taðkira (f)	تذكرة
air ticket	taðkirat ṭā'ira (f)	تذكرة طائرة
guidebook	dalīl (m)	دليل
map (tourist ~)	xarīṭa (f)	خريطة
area (rural ~)	mintaqa (f)	منطقة
place, site	makān (m)	مكان
exotica (n)	ɣarāba (f)	غرابة
exotic (adj)	ɣarīb	غريب
amazing (adj)	mudhiʃ	مدهش
group	maʒmū'a (f)	مجموعة
excursion, sightseeing tour	ʒawla (f)	جولة
guide (person)	murʃid (m)	مرشد

21. Hotel

hotel	funduq (m)	فندق
motel	mutīl (m)	موتيل
three-star (~ hotel)	θalāθat nuʒūm	ثلاثة نجوم

five-star	χamsat nuӡūm	خمسة نجوم
to stay (in a hotel, etc.)	nazal	نزل
room	γurfa (f)	غرفة
single room	γurfa li ʃaχs̩ wāḥid (f)	غرفة لشخص واحد
double room	γurfa li ʃaχs̩ayn (f)	غرفة لشخصين
to book a room	ḥaӡaz γurfa	حجز غرفة
half board	waӡbitān fil yawm (du)	وجبتان في اليوم
full board	θalāθ waӡabāt fil yawm	ثلاث وجبات في اليوم
with bath	bi ḥawḍ al istiḥmām	بحوض الإستحمام
with shower	bid duʃ	بالدوش
satellite television	tilivizyūn faḍā'iy (m)	تلفزيون فضائيّ
air-conditioner	takyīf (m)	تكييف
towel	fūta (f)	فوطة
key	miftāḥ (m)	مفتاح
administrator	mudīr (m)	مدير
chambermaid	'āmilat tanzīf γuraf (f)	عاملة تنظيف غرف
porter	ḥammāl (m)	حمّال
doorman	bawwāb (m)	بوّاب
restaurant	maṭ'am (m)	مطعم
pub, bar	bār (m)	بار
breakfast	fuṭūr (m)	فطور
dinner	'aʃā' (m)	عشاء
buffet	bufīh (m)	بوفيه
lobby	radha (f)	ردهة
lift	miṣ'ad (m)	مصعد
DO NOT DISTURB	ar raӡā' 'adam al iz'āӡ	الرجاء عدم الإزعاج
NO SMOKING	mamnū' at tadχīn	ممنوع التدخين

22. Sightseeing

monument	timθāl (m)	تمثال
fortress	qal'a (f), ḥiṣn (m)	قلعة، حصن
palace	qaṣr (m)	قصر
castle	qal'a (f)	قلعة
tower	burӡ (m)	برج
mausoleum	ḍarīḥ (m)	ضريح
architecture	handasa mi'māriyya (f)	هندسة معماريّة
medieval (adj)	min al qurūn al wusṭa	من القرون الوسطى
ancient (adj)	qadīm	قديم
national (adj)	waṭaniy	وطنيّ
famous (monument, etc.)	maʃhūr	مشهور
tourist	sā'iḥ (m)	سائح
guide (person)	murʃid (m)	مرشد
excursion, sightseeing tour	ӡawla (f)	جولة
to show (vt)	'araḍ	عرض

to tell (vt)	ḥaddaθ	حدّث
to find (vt)	waʒad	وجد
to get lost (lose one's way)	ḍāʿ	ضاع
map (e.g. underground ~)	χarîṭa (f)	خريطة
map (e.g. city ~)	χarîṭa (f)	خريطة
souvenir, gift	tiðkār (m)	تذكار
gift shop	maḥall hadāya (m)	محلّ هدايا
to take pictures	ṣawwar	صوّر
to have one's picture taken	taṣawwar	تصوّر

TRANSPORT

23. Airport

airport	maṭār (m)	مطار
aeroplane	ṭā'ira (f)	طائرة
airline	ʃarikat ṭayarān (f)	شركة طيران
air traffic controller	marāqib al ḥaraka	مراقب الحركة الجويّة
	al ʒawwiyya (pl)	

departure	muɣādara (f)	مغادرة
arrival	wuṣūl (m)	وصول
to arrive (by plane)	waṣal	وصل

| departure time | waqt al muɣādara (m) | وقت المغادرة |
| arrival time | waqt al wuṣūl (m) | وقت الوصول |

| to be delayed | ta'axxar | تأخّر |
| flight delay | ta'axxur ar riḥla (m) | تأخّر الرحلة |

information board	lawḥat al ma'lūmāt (f)	لوحة المعلومات
information	isti'lāmāt (pl)	إستعلامات
to announce (vt)	a'lan	أعلن
flight (e.g. next ~)	riḥla (f)	رحلة

| customs | ʒamārik (pl) | جمارك |
| customs officer | muwazzaf al ʒamārik (m) | موظّف الجمارك |

customs declaration	taṣrīḥ ʒumrukiy (m)	تصريح جمركيّ
to fill in (vt)	mala'	ملأ
to fill in the declaration	mala' at taṣrīḥ	ملأ التصريح
passport control	taftīʃ al ʒawāzāt (m)	تفتيش الجوازات

luggage	aʃ ʃunaṭ (pl)	الشنط
hand luggage	ʃunaṭ al yad (pl)	شنط اليد
luggage trolley	'arabat ʃunaṭ (f)	عربة شنط

landing	hubūṭ (m)	هبوط
landing strip	mamarr al hubūṭ (m)	ممرّ الهبوط
to land (vi)	habaṭ	هبط
airstair (passenger stair)	sullam aṭ ṭā'ira (m)	سلّم الطائرة

check-in	tasʒīl (m)	تسجيل
check-in counter	makān at tasʒīl (m)	مكان التسجيل
to check-in (vi)	saʒʒal	سجّل
boarding card	biṭāqat ṣu'ūd (f)	بطاقة صعود
departure gate	bawwābat al muɣādara (f)	بوّابة المغادرة

| transit | tranzīt (m) | ترانزيت |
| to wait (vt) | intazar | إنتظر |

departure lounge	qā'at al muɣādara (f)	قاعة المغادرة
to see off	wadda'	ودّع
to say goodbye	wadda'	ودّع

24. Aeroplane

aeroplane	ṭā'ira (f)	طائرة
air ticket	taðkirat ṭā'ira (f)	تذكرة طائرة
airline	ʃarikat ṭayarān (f)	شركة طيران
airport	maṭār (m)	مطار
supersonic (adj)	xāriq liṣ ṣawt	خارق للصوت

captain	qā'id aṭ ṭā'ira (m)	قائد الطائرة
crew	ṭāqim (m)	طاقم
pilot	ṭayyār (m)	طيّار
stewardess	muḍīfat ṭayarān (f)	مضيفة طيران
navigator	mallāḥ (m)	ملّاح

wings	aʒniḥa (pl)	أجنحة
tail	ðayl (m)	ذيل
cockpit	kabīna (f)	كابينة
engine	mutūr (m)	موتور

| undercarriage (landing gear) | 'aʒalāt al hubūṭ (pl) | عجلات الهبوط |
| turbine | turbīna (f) | تربينة |

| propeller | mirwaḥa (f) | مروحة |
| black box | musaʒʒil aṭ ṭayarān (m) | مسجّل الطيران |

| yoke (control column) | 'aʒalat qiyāda (f) | عجلة قيادة |
| fuel | wuqūd (m) | وقود |

safety card	biṭāqat as salāma (f)	بطاقة السلامة
oxygen mask	qinā' uksiʒīn (m)	قناع أوكسيجين
uniform	libās muwaḥḥad (m)	لباس موحّد

| lifejacket | sutrat naʒāt (f) | سترة نجاة |
| parachute | miẓallat hubūṭ (f) | مظلّة هبوط |

takeoff	iqlā' (m)	إقلاع
to take off (vi)	aqla'at	أقلعت
runway	madraʒ aṭ ṭā'irāt (m)	مدرج الطائرات

| visibility | ru'ya (f) | رؤية |
| flight (act of flying) | ṭayarān (m) | طيران |

| altitude | irtifā' (m) | إرتفاع |
| air pocket | ʒayb hawā'iy (m) | جيب هوائيّ |

seat	maq'ad (m)	مقعد
headphones	sammā'āt ra'siya (pl)	سمّاعات رأسيّة
folding tray (tray table)	ṣīniyya qābila liṭ ṭayy (f)	صينية قابلة للطيّ
airplane window	ʃubbāk aṭ ṭā'ira (m)	شبّاك الطائرة
aisle	mamarr (m)	ممرّ

25. Train

train	qiṭār (m)	قطار
commuter train	qiṭār (m)	قطار
express train	qiṭār sarī' (m)	قطار سريع
diesel locomotive	qāṭirat dīzil (f)	قاطرة ديزل
steam locomotive	qāṭira buχāriyya (f)	قاطرة بخاريّة
coach, carriage	'araba (f)	عربة
buffet car	'arabat al maṭ'am (f)	عربة المطعم
rails	quḍubān (pl)	قضبان
railway	sikka ḥadīdiyya (f)	سكة حديديّة
sleeper (track support)	'āriḍa (f)	عارضة
platform (railway ~)	raṣīf (m)	رصيف
platform (~ 1, 2, etc.)	χaṭṭ (m)	خطّ
semaphore	simafūr (m)	سيمافور
station	maḥaṭṭa (f)	محطّة
train driver	sā'iq (m)	سائق
porter (of luggage)	ḥammāl (m)	حمّال
carriage attendant	mas'ūl 'arabat al qiṭār (m)	مسؤول عربة القطار
passenger	rākib (m)	راكب
ticket inspector	kamsariy (m)	كمسريّ
corridor (in train)	mamarr (m)	ممرّ
emergency brake	farāmil aṭ ṭawāri' (pl)	فرامل الطوارئ
compartment	ɣurfa (f)	غرفة
berth	sarīr (m)	سرير
upper berth	sarīr 'ulwiy (m)	سرير علويّ
lower berth	sarīr sufliy (m)	سرير سفليّ
bed linen, bedding	aɣṭiyat as sarīr (pl)	أغطية السرير
ticket	taðkira (f)	تذكرة
timetable	ʒadwal (m)	جدول
information display	lawḥat ma'lūmāt (f)	لوحة معلومات
to leave, to depart	ɣādar	غادر
departure (of a train)	muɣādara (f)	مغادرة
to arrive (ab. train)	waṣal	وصل
arrival	wuṣūl (m)	وصول
to arrive by train	waṣal bil qiṭār	وصل بالقطار
to get on the train	rakib al qiṭār	ركب القطار
to get off the train	nazil min al qiṭār	نزل من القطار
train crash	hiṭām qiṭār (m)	حطام قطار
to derail (vi)	χaraʒ 'an χaṭṭ sayrih	خرج عن خطّ سيره
steam locomotive	qāṭira buχāriyya (f)	قاطرة بخاريّة
stoker, fireman	'aṭaʃʒiy (m)	عطشجيّ
firebox	furn al muḥarrik (m)	فرن المحرّك
coal	faḥm (m)	فحم

26. Ship

ship	safīna (f)	سفينة
vessel	safīna (f)	سفينة
steamship	bāxira (f)	باخرة
riverboat	bāxira nahriyya (f)	باخرة نهريّة
cruise ship	bāxira siyahiyya (f)	باخرة سياحيّة
cruiser	ṭarrād (m)	طرّاد
yacht	yaxt (m)	يخت
tugboat	qāṭira (f)	قاطرة
barge	ṣandal (m)	صندل
ferry	'abbāra (f)	عبّارة
sailing ship	safīna ʃirā'iyya (m)	سفينة شراعيّة
brigantine	markab ʃirā'iy (m)	مركب شراعيّ
ice breaker	muhaṭṭimat ʒalīd (f)	محطّمة جليد
submarine	ɣawwāṣa (f)	غوّاصة
boat (flat-bottomed ~)	markab (m)	مركب
dinghy (lifeboat)	zawraq (m)	زورق
lifeboat	qārib naʒāt (m)	قارب نجاة
motorboat	lanʃ (m)	لنش
captain	qubṭān (m)	قبطان
seaman	bahhār (m)	بحّار
sailor	bahhār (m)	بحّار
crew	ṭāqim (m)	طاقم
boatswain	raʾīs al bahhāra (m)	رئيس البحّارة
ship's boy	ṣabiy as safīna (m)	صبي السفينة
cook	ṭabbāx (m)	طبّاخ
ship's doctor	ṭabīb as safīna (m)	طبيب السفينة
deck	saṭh as safīna (m)	سطح السفينة
mast	sāriya (f)	سارية
sail	ʃirā' (m)	شراع
hold	'ambar (m)	عنبر
bow (prow)	muqaddama (m)	مقدّمة
stern	mu'axirat as safīna (f)	مؤخّرة السفينة
oar	miʒðāf (m)	مجذاف
screw propeller	mirwaha (f)	مروحة
cabin	kabīna (f)	كابينة
wardroom	ɣurfat al istirāha (f)	غرفة الإستراحة
engine room	qism al 'ālāt (m)	قسم الآلات
bridge	burʒ al qiyāda (m)	برج القيادة
radio room	ɣurfat al lāsilkiy (f)	غرفة اللاسلكيّ
wave (radio)	mawʒa (f)	موجة
logbook	siʒil as safīna (m)	سجل السفينة
spyglass	minẓār (m)	منظار
bell	ʒaras (m)	جرس

flag	'alam (m)	علم
hawser (mooring ~)	ḥabl (m)	حبل
knot (bowline, etc.)	'uqda (f)	عقدة

| deckrails | drabizīn (m) | درابزين |
| gangway | sullam (m) | سلّم |

anchor	mirsāt (f)	مرساة
to weigh anchor	rafa' mirsāt	رفع مرساة
to drop anchor	rasa	رسا
anchor chain	silsilat mirsāt (f)	سلسلة مرساة

port (harbour)	mīnā' (m)	ميناء
quay, wharf	marsa (m)	مرسى
to berth (moor)	rasa	رسا
to cast off	aqla'	أقلع

trip, voyage	riḥla (f)	رحلة
cruise (sea trip)	riḥla baḥriyya (f)	رحلة بحرية
course (route)	masār (m)	مسار
route (itinerary)	ṭarīq (m)	طريق

fairway (safe water channel)	maʒra milāḥiy (m)	مجرى ملاحيّ
shallows	miyāh ḍaḥla (f)	مياه ضحلة
to run aground	ʒanaḥ	جنح

storm	'āṣifa (f)	عاصفة
signal	iʃāra (f)	إشارة
to sink (vi)	ɣariq	غرق
Man overboard!	saqaṭ raʒul min as safīna!	سقط رجل من السفينة!
SOS (distress signal)	nidā' iɣāθa (m)	نداء إغاثة
ring buoy	ṭawq naʒāt (m)	طوق نجاة

CITY

27. Urban transport

bus, coach	bāṣ (m)	باص
tram	trām (m)	ترام
trolleybus	truli bāṣ (m)	ترولي باص
route (bus ~)	χaṭṭ (m)	خطّ
number (e.g. bus ~)	raqm (m)	رقم
to go by …	rakib …	ركب...
to get on (~ the bus)	rakib	ركب
to get off …	nazil min	نزل من
stop (e.g. bus ~)	mawqif (m)	موقف
next stop	al maḥaṭṭa al qādima (f)	المحطّة القادمة
terminus	āχir maḥaṭṭa (f)	آخر محطّة
timetable	ʒadwal (m)	جدول
to wait (vt)	intazar	إنتظر
ticket	taðkira (f)	تذكرة
fare	uʒra (f)	أجرة
cashier (ticket seller)	ṣarrāf (m)	صرّاف
ticket inspection	taftīʃ taðkira (m)	تفتيش تذكرة
ticket inspector	mufattiʃ taðākir (m)	مفتّش تذاكر
to be late (for …)	ta'aχχar	تأخّر
to miss (~ the train, etc.)	ta'aχχar	تأخّر
to be in a hurry	ista'ʒal	إستعجل
taxi, cab	taksi (m)	تاكسي
taxi driver	sā'iq taksi (m)	سائق تاكسي
by taxi	bit taksi	بالتاكسي
taxi rank	mawqif taksi (m)	موقف تاكسي
to call a taxi	kallam tāksi	كلّم تاكسي
to take a taxi	aχað taksi	أخذ تاكسي
traffic	ḥarakat al murūr (f)	حركة المرور
traffic jam	zaḥmat al murūr (f)	زحمة المرور
rush hour	sā'at að ðurwa (f)	ساعة الذروة
to park (vi)	awqaf	أوقف
to park (vt)	awqaf	أوقف
car park	mawqif as sayyārāt (m)	موقف السيارات
underground, tube	mitru (m)	مترو
station	maḥaṭṭa (f)	محطّة
to take the tube	rakib al mitru	ركب المترو
train	qiṭār (m)	قطار
train station	maḥaṭṭat qiṭār (f)	محطّة قطار

28. City. Life in the city

city, town	madīna (f)	مدينة
capital city	ʻāṣima (f)	عاصمة
village	qarya (f)	قرية

city map	xarīṭat al madīna (f)	خريطة المدينة
city centre	markaz al madīna (m)	مركز المدينة
suburb	ḍāḥiya (f)	ضاحية
suburban (adj)	aḍ ḍawāḥi	الضواحي

outskirts	aṭrāf al madīna (pl)	أطراف المدينة
environs (suburbs)	ḍawāḥi al madīna (pl)	ضواحي المدينة
city block	ḥayy (m)	حي
residential block (area)	ḥayy sakaniy (m)	حي سكني

traffic	ḥarakat al murūr (f)	حركة المرور
traffic lights	iʃārāt al murūr (pl)	إشارات المرور
public transport	wasāʼil an naql (pl)	وسائل النقل
crossroads	taqāṭuʻ (m)	تقاطع

zebra crossing	maʻbar al muʃāt (m)	معبر المشاة
pedestrian subway	nafaq muʃāt (m)	نفق مشاة
to cross (~ the street)	ʻabar	عبر
pedestrian	māʃi (m)	ماش
pavement	raṣīf (m)	رصيف

bridge	ʒisr (m)	جسر
embankment (river walk)	kurnīʃ (m)	كورنيش
fountain	nāfūra (f)	نافورة

allée (garden walkway)	mamʃa (m)	ممشى
park	ḥadīqa (f)	حديقة
boulevard	bulvār (m)	بولفار
square	maydān (m)	ميدان
avenue (wide street)	ʃāriʻ (m)	شارع
street	ʃāriʻ (m)	شارع
side street	zuqāq (m)	زقاق
dead end	ṭarīq masdūd (m)	طريق مسدود

house	bayt (m)	بيت
building	mabna (m)	مبنى
skyscraper	nāṭiḥat saḥāb (f)	ناطحة سحاب

facade	wāʒiha (f)	واجهة
roof	saqf (m)	سقف
window	ʃubbāk (m)	شبّاك
arch	qaws (m)	قوس
column	ʻamūd (m)	عمود
corner	zāwiya (f)	زاوية

shop window	vatrīna (f)	فترينة
signboard (store sign, etc.)	lāfita (f)	لافتة
poster (e.g., playbill)	mulṣaq (m)	ملصق
advertising poster	mulṣaq iʻlāniy (m)	ملصق إعلاني

hoarding	lawḥat i'lānāt (f)	لوحة إعلانات
rubbish	zubāla (f)	زبالة
rubbish bin	ṣundūq zubāla (m)	صندوق زبالة
to litter (vi)	rama zubāla	رمى زبالة
rubbish dump	mazbala (f)	مزبلة

telephone box	kuʃk tilifūn (m)	كشك تليفون
lamppost	'amūd al miṣbāḥ (m)	عمود المصباح
bench (park ~)	dikka (f), kursiy (m)	دكّة، كرسيّ

police officer	ʃurṭiy (m)	شرطيّ
police	ʃurṭa (f)	شرطة
beggar	ʃaḥḥāð (m)	شحّاذ
homeless (n)	mutaʃarrid (m)	متشرّد

29. Urban institutions

shop	maḥall (m)	محلّ
chemist, pharmacy	ṣaydaliyya (f)	صيدليّة
optician (spectacles shop)	al adawāt al baṣariyya (pl)	الأدوات البصريّة
shopping centre	markaz tiʒāriy (m)	مركز تجاريّ
supermarket	subirmarkit (m)	سوبرماركت

bakery	maxbaz (m)	مخبز
baker	xabbāz (m)	خبّاز
cake shop	dukkān ḥalawāniy (m)	دكّان حلوانيّ
grocery shop	baqqāla (f)	بقّالة
butcher shop	malḥama (f)	ملحمة

| greengrocer | dukkān xuḍār (m) | دكّان خضار |
| market | sūq (f) | سوق |

coffee bar	kafé (m), maqha (m)	كافيه، مقهى
restaurant	maṭ'am (m)	مطعم
pub, bar	ḥāna (f)	حانة
pizzeria	maṭ'am pizza (m)	مطعم بيتزا

hairdresser	ṣālūn ḥilāqa (m)	صالون حلاقة
post office	maktab al barīd (m)	مكتب البريد
dry cleaners	tanzīf ʒāff (m)	تنظيف جافّ
photo studio	istūdiyu taṣwīr (m)	إستوديو تصوير

shoe shop	maḥall aḥðiya (m)	محلّ أحذية
bookshop	maḥall kutub (m)	محلّ كتب
sports shop	maḥall riyāḍiy (m)	محلّ رياضيّ

clothes repair shop	maḥall xiyāṭat malābis (m)	محلّ خياطة ملابس
formal wear hire	maḥall ta'ʒīr malābis rasmiyya (m)	محلّ تأجير ملابس رسمية
video rental shop	maḥal ta'ʒīr vidiyu (m)	محلّ تأجير فيديو

circus	sirk (m)	سيرك
zoo	ḥadīqat al ḥayawān (f)	حديقة حيوان
cinema	sinima (f)	سينما

museum	matḥaf (m)	متحف
library	maktaba (f)	مكتبة
theatre	masraḥ (m)	مسرح
opera (opera house)	ubra (f)	أوبرا
nightclub	malha layliy (m)	ملهى ليلي
casino	kazinu (m)	كازينو
mosque	masʒid (m)	مسجد
synagogue	kanīs ma'bad yahūdiy (m)	كنيس معبد يهودي
cathedral	katidrā'iyya (f)	كاتدرائية
temple	ma'bad (m)	معبد
church	kanīsa (f)	كنيسة
college	kulliyya (m)	كلّية
university	ʒāmi'a (f)	جامعة
school	madrasa (f)	مدرسة
prefecture	muqāṭa'a (f)	مقاطعة
town hall	baladiyya (f)	بلدّية
hotel	funduq (m)	فندق
bank	bank (m)	بنك
embassy	safāra (f)	سفارة
travel agency	ʃarikat siyāḥa (f)	شركة سياحة
information office	maktab al isti'lāmāt (m)	مكتب الإستعلامات
currency exchange	ṣarrāfa (f)	صرّافة
underground, tube	mitru (m)	مترو
hospital	mustaʃfa (m)	مستشفى
petrol station	maḥaṭṭat banzīn (f)	محطة بنزين
car park	mawqif as sayyārāt (m)	موقف السيّارات

30. Signs

signboard (store sign, etc.)	lāfita (f)	لافتة
notice (door sign, etc.)	bayān (m)	بيان
poster	mulṣaq i'lāniy (m)	ملصق إعلاني
direction sign	'alāmat ittiʒāh (f)	علامة إتجاه
arrow (sign)	'alāmat iʃāra (f)	علامة إشارة
caution	taḥðīr (m)	تحذير
warning sign	lāfitat taḥðīr (f)	لافتة تحذير
to warn (vt)	ḥaððar	حذّر
rest day (weekly ~)	yawm 'uṭla (m)	يوم عطلة
timetable (schedule)	ʒadwal (m)	جدول
opening hours	awqāt al 'amal (pl)	أوقات العمل
WELCOME!	ahlan wa sahlan!	أهلًا وسهلًا
ENTRANCE	duxūl	دخول
WAY OUT	xurūʒ	خروج
PUSH	idfa'	إدفع

PULL	isḥab	إسحب
OPEN	maftūḥ	مفتوح
CLOSED	muɣlaq	مغلق

WOMEN	lis sayyidāt	للسيدات
MEN	lir riǧāl	للرجال

DISCOUNTS	ҳaṣm	خصم
SALE	taҳfīḍāt	تخفيضات
NEW!	ǧadīd!	جديد!
FREE	maǧǧānan	مجّانًا

ATTENTION!	intibāh!	إنتباه!
NO VACANCIES	kull al amākin maḥǧūza	كل الأماكن محجوزة
RESERVED	maḥǧūz	محجوز

ADMINISTRATION	idāra	إدارة
STAFF ONLY	lil ʿāmilīn faqaṭ	للعاملين فقط

BEWARE OF THE DOG!	iḥðar wuǧūd al kalb	إحذر وجود الكلب
NO SMOKING	mamnūʿ at tadҳīn	ممنوع التدخين
DO NOT TOUCH!	ʿadam al lams	عدم اللمس

DANGEROUS	ҳaṭīr	خطير
DANGER	ҳaṭar	خطر
HIGH VOLTAGE	tayyār ʿāli	تيّار عالي
NO SWIMMING!	as sibāḥa mamnūʿa	السباحة ممنوعة
OUT OF ORDER	muʿaṭṭal	معطّل

FLAMMABLE	sarīʿ al iʃtiʿāl	سريع الإشتعال
FORBIDDEN	mamnūʿ	ممنوع
NO TRESPASSING!	mamnūʿ al murūr	ممنوع المرور
WET PAINT	iḥðar ṭilāʾ ɣayr ǧāff	إحذر طلاء غير جاف

31. Shopping

to buy (purchase)	iʃtara	إشترى
shopping	ʃayʾ (m)	شيء
to go shopping	iʃtara	إشترى
shopping	ʃubinɣ (m)	شوبينغ

to be open (ab. shop)	maftūḥ	مفتوح
to be closed	muɣlaq	مغلق

footwear, shoes	aḥðiya (pl)	أحذية
clothes, clothing	malābis (pl)	ملابس
cosmetics	mawādd at taǧmīl (pl)	موادّ التجميل
food products	maʾkūlāt (pl)	مأكولات
gift, present	hadiyya (f)	هديّة

shop assistant (masc.)	bāʾiʿ (m)	بائع
shop assistant (fem.)	bāʾiʿa (f)	بائعة
cash desk	ṣundūʾ ad dafʿ (m)	صندوق الدفع
mirror	mirʾāt (f)	مرآة

| counter (shop ~) | minḍada (f) | منضدة |
| fitting room | ɣurfat al qiyās (f) | غرفة القياس |

to try on	ʒarrab	جرّب
to fit (ab. dress, etc.)	nāsab	ناسب
to fancy (vt)	aʻʒab	أعجب

price	siʻr (m)	سعر
price tag	tikit as siʻr (m)	تيكت السعر
to cost (vt)	kallaf	كلف
How much?	bikam?	بكم؟
discount	xaṣm (m)	خصم

inexpensive (adj)	ɣayr ɣāli	غير غال
cheap (adj)	raxīṣ	رخيص
expensive (adj)	ɣāli	غال
It's expensive	haða ɣāli	هذا غال

hire (n)	istiʼʒār (m)	إستئجار
to hire (~ a dinner jacket)	staʼʒar	إستأجر
credit (trade credit)	iʼtimān (m)	إئتمان
on credit (adv)	bid dayn	بالدين

CLOTHING & ACCESSORIES

32. Outerwear. Coats

clothes	malābis (pl)	ملابس
outerwear	malābis fawqāniyya (pl)	ملابس فوقانيّة
winter clothing	malābis ʃitawiyya (pl)	ملابس شتويّة
coat (overcoat)	miʿṭaf (m)	معطف
fur coat	miʿtaf farw (m)	معطف فرو
fur jacket	ʒakīt farw (m)	جاكيت فرو
down coat	ḥaʃiyyat rīʃ (m)	حشية ريش
jacket (e.g. leather ~)	ʒākīt (m)	جاكيت
raincoat (trenchcoat, etc.)	miʿṭaf lil maṭar (m)	معطف للمطر
waterproof (adj)	ṣāmid lil mā'	صامد للماء

33. Men's & women's clothing

shirt (button shirt)	qamīṣ (m)	قميص
trousers	banṭalūn (m)	بنطلون
jeans	ʒīnz (m)	جينز
suit jacket	sutra (f)	سترة
suit	badla (f)	بدلة
dress (frock)	fustān (m)	فستان
skirt	tannūra (f)	تنّورة
blouse	blūza (f)	بلوزة
knitted jacket (cardigan, etc.)	kardigān (m)	كارديجان
jacket (of a woman's suit)	ʒākīt (m)	جاكيت
T-shirt	ti ʃīrt (m)	تي شيرت
shorts (short trousers)	ʃūrt (m)	شورت
tracksuit	badlat at tadrīb (f)	بدلة التدريب
bathrobe	θawb ḥammām (m)	ثوب حمّام
pyjamas	biʒāma (f)	بيجاما
jumper (sweater)	bulūvir (m)	بلوفر
pullover	bulūvir (m)	بلوفر
waistcoat	ṣudayriy (m)	صديريّ
tailcoat	badlat sahra (f)	بدلة سهرة
dinner suit	smūkin (m)	سموكن
uniform	zayy muwaḥḥad (m)	زي موحّد
workwear	θiyāb al ʿamal (m)	ثياب العمل
boiler suit	uvirūl (m)	اوفرول
coat (e.g. doctor's smock)	θawb (m)	ثوب

34. Clothing. Underwear

underwear	malābis dāḵiliyya (pl)	ملابس داخليّة
pants	sirwāl dāḵiliy riӡāliy (m)	سروال داخلي رجاليّ
panties	sirwāl dāḵiliy nisā'iy (m)	سروال داخليّ نسائيّ
vest (singlet)	qamīṣ bila aqmām (m)	قميص بلا أكمام
socks	ӡawārib (pl)	جوارب
nightdress	qamīṣ nawm (m)	قميص نوم
bra	ḥammālat ṣadr (f)	حمّالة صدر
knee highs (knee-high socks)	ӡawārib ṭawīla (pl)	جوارب طويلة
tights	ӡawārib kulūn (pl)	جوارب كولون
stockings (hold ups)	ӡawārib nisā'iyya (pl)	جوارب نسائية
swimsuit, bikini	libās sibāḥa (m)	لباس سباحة

35. Headwear

hat	qubba'a (f)	قبّعة
trilby hat	burnayṭa (f)	برنيطة
baseball cap	kāb baysbūl (m)	كاب بيسبول
flatcap	qubba'a musaṭṭaḥa (f)	قبّعة مسطحة
beret	birīh (m)	بيريه
hood	ɣiṭā' (m)	غطاء
panama hat	qubba'at banāma (f)	قبّعة بناما
knit cap (knitted hat)	qubbā'a maḥbūka (m)	قبّعة محبوكة
headscarf	'iʃārb (m)	إيشارب
women's hat	burnayṭa (f)	برنيطة
hard hat	ḵūða (f)	خوذة
forage cap	kāb (m)	كاب
helmet	ḵūða (f)	خوذة
bowler	qubba'at dirbi (f)	قبّعة ديربي
top hat	qubba'a 'āliya (f)	قبّعة عالية

36. Footwear

footwear	aḥðiya (pl)	أحذية
shoes (men's shoes)	ӡazma (f)	جزمة
shoes (women's shoes)	ӡazma (f)	جزمة
boots (e.g., cowboy ~)	būt (m)	بوت
carpet slippers	ʃibʃib (m)	شبشب
trainers	ḥiðā' riyāḍiy (m)	حذاء رياضيّ
trainers	kutʃi (m)	كوتشي
sandals	ṣandal (pl)	صندل
cobbler (shoe repairer)	iskāfiy (m)	إسكافيّ
heel	ka'b (m)	كعب

pair (of shoes)	zawʒ (m)	زوج
lace (shoelace)	ʃarīṭ (m)	شريط
to lace up (vt)	rabaṭ	ربط
shoehorn	labbāsat ḥiðā' (f)	لبّاسة حذاء
shoe polish	warnīʃ al ḥiðā' (m)	ورنيش الحذاء

37. Personal accessories

gloves	quffāz (m)	قفّاز
mittens	quffāz muɣlaq (m)	قفّاز مغلق
scarf (muffler)	ʔiʃārb (m)	إيشارب
glasses	nazzāra (f)	نظّارة
frame (eyeglass ~)	iṭār (m)	إطار
umbrella	ʃamsiyya (f)	شمسيّة
walking stick	'aṣa (f)	عصا
hairbrush	furʃat ʃa'r (f)	فرشة شعر
fan	mirwaḥa yadawiyya (f)	مروحة يدويّة
tie (necktie)	karavatta (f)	كرافتة
bow tie	babyūn (m)	ببيون
braces	ḥammāla (f)	حمّالة
handkerchief	mandīl (m)	منديل
comb	miʃṭ (m)	مشط
hair slide	dabbūs (m)	دبّوس
hairpin	bansa (m)	بنسة
buckle	bukla (f)	بكلة
belt	ḥizām (m)	حزام
shoulder strap	ḥammalat al katf (f)	حمّالة الكتف
bag (handbag)	ʃanṭa (f)	شنطة
handbag	ʃanṭat yad (f)	شنطة يد
rucksack	ḥaqībat ẓahr (f)	حقيبة ظهر

38. Clothing. Miscellaneous

fashion	mūḍa (f)	موضة
in vogue (adj)	fil mūḍa	في الموضة
fashion designer	muṣammim azyā' (m)	مصمّم أزياء
collar	yāqa (f)	ياقة
pocket	ʒayb (m)	جيب
pocket (as adj)	ʒayb	جيب
sleeve	kumm (m)	كمّ
hanging loop	'allāqa (f)	علّاقة
flies (on trousers)	lisān (m)	لسان
zip (fastener)	zimām munzaliq (m)	زمام منزلق
fastener	miʃbak (m)	مشبك
button	zirr (m)	زرّ

buttonhole	'urwa (f)	عروة
to come off (ab. button)	waqa'	وقع
to sew (vi, vt)	xāṭ	خاط
to embroider (vi, vt)	ṭarraz	طرّز
embroidery	taṭrīz (m)	تطريز
sewing needle	ibra (f)	إبرة
thread	xayṭ (m)	خيط
seam	darz (m)	درز
to get dirty (vi)	tawassax	توسّخ
stain (mark, spot)	buq'a (f)	بقعة
to crease, to crumple	takarmaʃ	تكرمش
to tear, to rip (vt)	qaṭṭa'	قطّع
clothes moth	'uθθa (f)	عثّة

39. Personal care. Cosmetics

toothpaste	ma'ʒūn asnān (m)	معجون أسنان
toothbrush	furʃat asnān (f)	فرشة أسنان
to clean one's teeth	nazzaf al asnān	نظف الأسنان
razor	mūs ḥilāqa (m)	موس حلاقة
shaving cream	krīm ḥilāqa (m)	كريم حلاقة
to shave (vi)	ḥalaq	حلق
soap	ṣābūn (m)	صابون
shampoo	ʃāmbū (m)	شامبو
scissors	maqaṣṣ (m)	مقصّ
nail file	mibrad (m)	مبرد
nail clippers	milqaṭ (m)	ملقط
tweezers	milqaṭ (m)	ملقط
cosmetics	mawādd at taʒmīl (pl)	موادّ التجميل
face mask	mask (m)	ماسك
manicure	manikūr (m)	مانيكور
to have a manicure	'amal manikūr	عمل مانيكور
pedicure	badikīr (m)	باديكير
make-up bag	ḥaqībat adawāt at taʒmīl (f)	حقيبة أدوات التجميل
face powder	budrat waʒh (f)	بودرة وجه
powder compact	'ulbat būdra (f)	علبة بودرة
blusher	aḥmar xudūd (m)	أحمر خدود
perfume (bottled)	'iṭr (m)	عطر
toilet water (lotion)	kulūnya (f)	كولونيا
lotion	lusiyun (m)	لوسيون
cologne	kulūniya (f)	كولونيا
eyeshadow	ay ʃaduw (m)	اي شادو
eyeliner	kuḥl al 'uyūn (m)	كحل العين
mascara	maskara (f)	ماسكارا
lipstick	aḥmar ʃifāh (m)	أحمر شفاه

nail polish	mulammi' al aẓāfir (m)	ملمّع الاظافر
hair spray	muθabbit aʃ ʃaʻr (m)	مثبّت الشعر
deodorant	muzīl rawā'iḥ (m)	مزيل روائح
cream	krīm (m)	كريم
face cream	krīm lil waʒh (m)	كريم للوجه
hand cream	krīm lil yadayn (m)	كريم لليدين
anti-wrinkle cream	krīm muḍādd lit taʒāʻīd (m)	كريم مضادّ للتجاعيد
day cream	krīm an nahār (m)	كريم النهار
night cream	krīm al layl (m)	كريم الليل
day (as adj)	nahāriy	نهاريّ
night (as adj)	layliy	ليلي
tampon	tambūn (m)	تانبون
toilet paper (toilet roll)	waraq ḥammām (m)	ورق حمّام
hair dryer	muʒaffif ʃaʻr (m)	مجفّف شعر

40. Watches. Clocks

watch (wristwatch)	sāʻa (f)	ساعة
dial	waʒh as sāʻa (m)	وجه الساعة
hand (clock, watch)	'aqrab as sāʻa (m)	عقرب الساعة
metal bracelet	siwār sāʻa maʻdaniyya (m)	سوار ساعة معدنية
watch strap	siwār sāʻa (m)	سوار ساعة
battery	baṭṭāriyya (f)	بطّاريّة
to be flat (battery)	tafarraɣ	تفرّغ
to change a battery	ɣayyar al baṭṭāriyya	غيّر البطّاريّة
to run fast	sabaq	سبق
to run slow	ta'axxar	تأخّر
wall clock	sāʻat ḥā'iṭ (f)	ساعة حائط
hourglass	sāʻa ramliyya (f)	ساعة رمليّة
sundial	sāʻa ʃamsiyya (f)	ساعة شمسيّة
alarm clock	munabbih (m)	منبّه
watchmaker	saʻātiy (m)	ساعاتيّ
to repair (vt)	aṣlaḥ	أصلح

EVERYDAY EXPERIENCE

41. Money

money	nuqūd (pl)	نقود
currency exchange	taḥwīl ‘umla (m)	تحويل عملة
exchange rate	si‘r aṣ ṣarf (m)	سعر الصرف
cashpoint	ṣarrāf ’āliy (m)	صرّاف آليّ
coin	qiṭ‘a naqdiyya (f)	قطعة نقديّة
dollar	dulār (m)	دولار
euro	yuru (m)	يورو
lira	lira iṭāliyya (f)	ليرة إيطالية
Deutschmark	mark almāniy (m)	مارك ألماني
franc	frank (m)	فرنك
pound sterling	ʒunayh istirlīniy (m)	جنيه استرلينيّ
yen	yīn (m)	ين
debt	dayn (m)	دين
debtor	mudīn (m)	مدين
to lend (money)	sallaf	سلّف
to borrow (vi, vt)	istalaf	إستلف
bank	bank (m)	بنك
account	ḥisāb (m)	حساب
to deposit (vt)	awda‘	أودع
to deposit into the account	awda‘ fil ḥisāb	أودع في الحساب
to withdraw (vt)	saḥab min al ḥisāb	سحب من الحساب
credit card	biṭāqat i’timān (f)	بطاقة إئتمان
cash	nuqūd (pl)	نقود
cheque	ʃīk (m)	شيك
to write a cheque	katab ʃīk	كتب شيكًا
chequebook	daftar ʃīkāt (m)	دفتر شيكات
wallet	maḥfaẓat ʒīb (f)	محفظة جيب
purse	maḥfaẓat fakka (f)	محفظة فكّة
safe	χizāna (f)	خزانة
heir	wāris (m)	وارث
inheritance	wirāθa (f)	وراثة
fortune (wealth)	θarwa (f)	ثروة
lease	ʔʒār (m)	إيجار
rent (money)	uʒrat as sakan (f)	أجرة السكن
to rent (sth from sb)	ista’ʒar	إستأجر
price	si‘r (m)	سعر
cost	θaman (m)	ثمن

sum	mablaɣ (m)	مبلغ
to spend (vt)	ṣaraf	صرف
expenses	maṣārīf (pl)	مصاريف
to economize (vi, vt)	waffar	وفّر
economical	muwaffir	موفّر
to pay (vi, vt)	dafaʿ	دفع
payment	dafʿ (m)	دفع
change (give the ~)	al bāqi (m)	الباقي
tax	ḍarība (f)	ضريبة
fine	ɣarāma (f)	غرامة
to fine (vt)	faraḍ ɣarāma	فرض غرامة

42. Post. Postal service

post office	maktab al barīd (m)	مكتب البريد
post (letters, etc.)	al barīd (m)	البريد
postman	sāʾi al barīd (m)	ساعي البريد
opening hours	awqāt al ʿamal (pl)	أوقات العمل
letter	risāla (f)	رسالة
registered letter	risāla musaʒʒala (f)	رسالة مسجّلة
postcard	biṭāqa barīdiyya (f)	بطاقة بريديّة
telegram	barqiyya (f)	برقيّة
parcel	ṭard (m)	طرد
money transfer	ḥawāla māliyya (f)	حوالة ماليّة
to receive (vt)	istalam	إستلم
to send (vt)	arsal	أرسل
sending	irsāl (m)	إرسال
address	ʿunwān (m)	عنوان
postcode	raqm al barīd (m)	رقم البريد
sender	mursil (m)	مرسل
receiver	mursal ilayh (m)	مرسل إليه
name (first name)	ism (m)	إسم
surname (last name)	ism al ʿāʾila (m)	إسم العائلة
postage rate	taʿrīfa (f)	تعريفة
standard (adj)	ʿādiy	عاديّ
economical (adj)	muwaffir	موفّر
weight	wazn (m)	وزن
to weigh (~ letters)	wazan	وزن
envelope	zarf (m)	ظرف
postage stamp	ṭābiʿ (m)	طابع
to stamp an envelope	alṣaq ṭābiʿ	ألصق طابعا

43. Banking

bank	bank (m)	بنك
branch (of a bank)	farʿ (m)	فرع

consultant	muwaẓẓaf bank (m)	موظف بنك
manager (director)	mudīr (m)	مدير
bank account	ḥisāb (m)	حساب
account number	raqm al ḥisāb (m)	رقم الحساب
current account	ḥisāb ӡāri (m)	حساب جار
deposit account	ḥisāb tawfīr (m)	حساب توفير
to open an account	fataḥ ḥisāb	فتح حسابا
to close the account	aɣlaq ḥisāb	أغلق حسابا
to deposit into the account	awda' fil ḥisāb	أودع في الحساب
to withdraw (vt)	saḥab min al ḥisāb	سحب من الحساب
deposit	wadī'a (f)	وديعة
to make a deposit	awda'	أودع
wire transfer	ḥawāla (f)	حوالة
to wire, to transfer	ḥawwal	حوّل
sum	mablaɣ (m)	مبلغ
How much?	kam?	كم؟
signature	tawqī' (m)	توقيع
to sign (vt)	waqqa'	وقّع
credit card	biṭāqat i'timān (f)	بطاقة ائتمان
code (PIN code)	kūd (m)	كود
credit card number	raqm biṭāqat i'timān (m)	رقم بطاقة إئتمان
cashpoint	ṣarrāf 'āliy (m)	صرّاف آليّ
cheque	ʃīk (m)	شيك
to write a cheque	katab ʃīk	كتب شيكًا
chequebook	daftar ʃīkāt (m)	دفتر شيكات
loan (bank ~)	qarḍ (m)	قرض
to apply for a loan	qaddam ṭalab lil ḥuṣūl 'ala qarḍ	قدم طلبا للحصول على قرض
to get a loan	ḥaṣal 'ala qarḍ	حصل على قرض
to give a loan	qaddam qarḍ	قدمُ قرضا
guarantee	ḍamān (m)	ضمان

44. Telephone. Phone conversation

telephone	hātif (m)	هاتف
mobile phone	hātif maḥmūl (m)	هاتف محمول
answerphone	muӡīb al hātif (m)	مجيب الهاتف
to call (by phone)	ittaṣal	إتّصل
call, ring	mukālama tilifuniyya (f)	مكالمة تليفونية
to dial a number	ittaṣal bi raqm	إتّصل برقم
Hello!	alu!	ألو!
to ask (vt)	sa'al	سأل
to answer (vi, vt)	radd	ردّ
to hear (vt)	sami'	سمع

well (adv)	ʒayyidan	جَيِّدًا
not well (adv)	sayyiʾan	سَيِّئًا
noises (interference)	taʃwīʃ (m)	تشويش
receiver	sammāʿa (f)	سمّاعة
to pick up (~ the phone)	rafaʿ as sammāʿa	رفع السمّاعة
to hang up (~ the phone)	qafal as sammāʿa	قفل السمّاعة
busy (engaged)	maʃɣūl	مشغول
to ring (ab. phone)	rann	رنّ
telephone book	dalīl at tilifūn (m)	دليل التليفون
local (adj)	mahalliyya	ة محلّية
local call	mukālama hātifiyya mahalliyya (f)	مكالمة هاتفيّة محلّيّة
trunk (e.g. ~ call)	baʿīd al mada	بعيد المدى
trunk call	mukālama baʿīdat al mada (f)	مكالمة بعيدة المدى
international (adj)	duwaliy	دولي
international call	mukālama duwaliyya (f)	مكالمة دوليّة

45. Mobile telephone

mobile phone	hātif mahmūl (m)	هاتف محمول
display	ʒihāz ʿard (m)	جهاز عرض
button	zirr (m)	زر
SIM card	sim kart (m)	سيم كارت
battery	battāriyya (f)	بطاريّة
to be flat (battery)	xalaṣat	خلصت
charger	ʃāhin (m)	شاحن
menu	qāʾima (f)	قائمة
settings	awdāʿ (pl)	أوضاع
tune (melody)	naɣma (f)	نغمة
to select (vt)	ixtār	إختار
calculator	ʾāla hāsiba (f)	آلة حاسبة
voice mail	barīd ṣawtiy (m)	بريد صوتي
alarm clock	munabbih (m)	منبّه
contacts	ʒihāt al ittiṣāl (pl)	جهات الإتّصال
SMS (text message)	risāla qaṣīra ɛsɛmɛs (f)	sms رسالة قصيرة
subscriber	muʃtarik (m)	مشترك

46. Stationery

ballpoint pen	qalam ʒāf (m)	قلم جاف
fountain pen	qalam rīʃa (m)	قلم ريشة
pencil	qalam ruṣāṣ (m)	قلم رصاص
highlighter	markir (m)	ماركر
felt-tip pen	qalam xaṭṭāt (m)	قلم خطاط

| notepad | muðakkira (f) | مذكّرة |
| diary | ӡadwal al a'māl (m) | جدول الأعمال |

ruler	masṭara (f)	مسطرة
calculator	'āla ḥāsiba (f)	آلة حاسبة
rubber	astīka (f)	استيكة
drawing pin	dabbūs (m)	دبّوس
paper clip	dabbūs waraq (m)	دبّوس ورق

glue	ṣamɣ (m)	صمغ
stapler	dabbāsa (f)	دبّاسة
hole punch	xarrāma (m)	خرّامة
pencil sharpener	mibrāt (f)	مبراة

47. Foreign languages

language	luɣa (f)	لغة
foreign (adj)	aӡnabiy	أجنبيّ
foreign language	luɣa aӡnabiyya (f)	لغة أجنبيّة
to study (vt)	daras	درس
to learn (language, etc.)	ta'allam	تعلّم

to read (vi, vt)	qara'	قرأ
to speak (vi, vt)	takallam	تكلّم
to understand (vt)	fahim	فهم
to write (vt)	katab	كتب

fast (adv)	bi sur'a	بسرعة
slowly (adv)	bi buṭ'	ببطء
fluently (adv)	bi ṭalāqa	بطلاقة

rules	qawā'id (pl)	قواعد
grammar	an naḥw waṣ ṣarf (m)	النحو والصرف
vocabulary	mufradāt al luɣa (pl)	مفردات اللغة
phonetics	ṣawtīyyāt (pl)	صوتيّات

textbook	kitāb ta'līm (m)	كتاب تعليم
dictionary	qāmūs (m)	قاموس
teach-yourself book	kitāb ta'līm ðātiy (m)	كتاب تعليم ذاتيّ
phrasebook	kitāb lil 'ibārāt aʃ ʃā'i'a (m)	كتاب للعبارت الشائعة

cassette, tape	ʃarīṭ (m)	شريط
videotape	ʃarīṭ vidiyu (m)	شريط فيديو
CD, compact disc	si di (m)	سي دي
DVD	di vi di (m)	دي في دي

alphabet	alifbā' (m)	الفباء
to spell (vt)	tahaӡӡa	تهجّى
pronunciation	nuṭq (m)	نطق

accent	lukna (f)	لكنة
with an accent	bi lukna	بلكنة
without an accent	bi dūn lukna	بدون لكنة
word	kalima (f)	كلمة

meaning	ma'na (m)	معنى
course (e.g. a French ~)	dawra (f)	دورة
to sign up	saʒʒal ismahu	سجّل إسمه
teacher	mudarris (m)	مدرّس
translation (process)	tarʒama (f)	ترجمة
translation (text, etc.)	tarʒama (f)	ترجمة
translator	mutarʒim (m)	مترجم
interpreter	mutarʒim fawriy (m)	مترجم فوري
polyglot	'alīm bi 'iddat luɣāt (m)	عليم بعدّة لغات
memory	ðākira (f)	ذاكرة

MEALS. RESTAURANT

48. Table setting

spoon	mil'aqa (f)	ملعقة
knife	sikkīn (m)	سكّين
fork	ʃawka (f)	شوكة
cup (e.g., coffee ~)	finʒān (m)	فنجان
plate (dinner ~)	ṭabaq (m)	طبق
saucer	ṭabaq finʒān (m)	طبق فنجان
serviette	mandīl (m)	منديل
toothpick	χallat asnān (f)	خلّة أسنان

49. Restaurant

restaurant	maṭ'am (m)	مطعم
coffee bar	kafé (m), maqha (m)	كافيه, مقهى
pub, bar	bār (m)	بار
tearoom	ṣālun ʃāy (m)	صالون شاي
waiter	nādil (m)	نادل
waitress	nādila (f)	نادلة
barman	bārman (m)	بارمان
menu	qā'imat aṭ ṭa'ām (f)	قائمة طعام
wine list	qā'imat al χumūr (f)	قائمة خمور
to book a table	haʒaz mā'ida	حجز مائدة
course, dish	waʒba (f)	وجبة
to order (meal)	ṭalab	طلب
to make an order	ṭalab	طلب
aperitif	ʃarāb (m)	شراب
starter	muqabbilāt (pl)	مقبّلات
dessert, pudding	halawiyyāt (pl)	حلويّات
bill	hisāb (m)	حساب
to pay the bill	dafa' al hisāb	دفع الحساب
to give change	a'ṭa al bāqi	أعطى الباقي
tip	baqʃīʃ (m)	بقشيش

50. Meals

food	akl (m)	أكل
to eat (vi, vt)	akal	أكل

breakfast	fuṭūr (m)	فطور
to have breakfast	afṭar	أفطر
lunch	ɣadā' (m)	غداء
to have lunch	taɣadda	تغدّى
dinner	'aʃā' (m)	عشاء
to have dinner	ta'aʃʃa	تعشّى
appetite	ʃahiyya (f)	شهيّة
Enjoy your meal!	hanī'an marī'an!	هنيئًا مريئًا!
to open (~ a bottle)	fataḥ	فتح
to spill (liquid)	dalaq	دلق
to spill out (vi)	indalaq	إندلق
to boil (vi)	ɣala	غلى
to boil (vt)	ɣala	غلى
boiled (~ water)	maɣliy	مغليّ
to chill, cool down (vt)	barrad	برّد
to chill (vi)	tabarrad	تبرّد
taste, flavour	ṭa'm (m)	طعم
aftertaste	al maðāq al 'āliq fil fam (m)	المذاق العالق فى الفم
to slim down (lose weight)	faqad al wazn	فقد الوزن
diet	ḥimya ɣaðā'iyya (f)	حمية غذائية
vitamin	vitamīn (m)	فيتامين
calorie	su'ra ḥarāriyya (f)	سعرة حراريّة
vegetarian (n)	nabātiy (m)	نباتيّ
vegetarian (adj)	nabātiy	نباتيّ
fats (nutrient)	duhūn (pl)	دهون
proteins	brutināt (pl)	بروتينات
carbohydrates	naʃawiyyāt (pl)	نشويّات
slice (of lemon, ham)	ʃarīḥa (f)	شريحة
piece (of cake, pie)	qiṭ'a (f)	قطعة
crumb (of bread, cake, etc.)	futāta (f)	فتاتة

51. Cooked dishes

course, dish	waʒba (f)	وجبة
cuisine	maṭbax (m)	مطبخ
recipe	waṣfa (f)	وصفة
portion	waʒba (f)	وجبة
salad	sulṭa (f)	سلطة
soup	ʃūrba (f)	شوربة
clear soup (broth)	maraq (m)	مرق
sandwich (bread)	sandawitʃ (m)	ساندويتش
fried eggs	bayḍ maqliy (m)	بيض مقليّ
hamburger (beefburger)	hamburger (m)	هامبرجر
beefsteak	biftīk (m)	بفتيك
side dish	ṭabaq ʒānibiy (m)	طبق جانبيّ

spaghetti	spaɣitti (m)	سباغيتي
mash	harīs baṭāṭis (m)	هريس بطاطس
pizza	bītza (f)	بيتزا
porridge (oatmeal, etc.)	ʿaṣīda (f)	عصيدة
omelette	bayḍ maxfūq (m)	بيض مخفوق

boiled (e.g. ~ beef)	maslūq	مسلوق
smoked (adj)	mudaxxin	مدخّن
fried (adj)	maqliy	مقلي
dried (adj)	muʒaffaf	مجفّف
frozen (adj)	muʒammad	مجمّد
pickled (adj)	muxallil	مخلّل

sweet (sugary)	musakkar	مسكّر
salty (adj)	māliḥ	مالح
cold (adj)	bārid	بارد
hot (adj)	sāxin	ساخن
bitter (adj)	murr	مرّ
tasty (adj)	laðīð	لذيذ

to cook in boiling water	ṭabax	طبخ
to cook (dinner)	ḥaḍḍar	حضّر
to fry (vt)	qala	قلي
to heat up (food)	saxxan	سخّن

to salt (vt)	mallaḥ	ملّح
to pepper (vt)	falfal	فلفل
to grate (vt)	baʃar	بشر
peel (n)	qiʃra (f)	قشرة
to peel (vt)	qaʃʃar	قشّر

52. Food

meat	laḥm (m)	لحم
chicken	daʒāʒ (m)	دجاج
poussin	farrūʒ (m)	فرّوج
duck	baṭṭa (f)	بطّة
goose	iwazza (f)	إوزّة
game	ṣayd (m)	صيد
turkey	daʒāʒ rūmiy (m)	دجاج رومي

pork	laḥm al xinzīr (m)	لحم الخنزير
veal	laḥm il ʿiʒl (m)	لحم العجل
lamb	laḥm aḍ ḍaʾn (m)	لحم الضأن
beef	laḥm al baqar (m)	لحم البقر
rabbit	arnab (m)	أرنب

sausage (bologna, etc.)	suʒuq (m)	سجق
vienna sausage (frankfurter)	suʒuq (m)	سجق
bacon	bikūn (m)	بيكون
ham	hām (m)	هام
gammon	faxð xinzīr (m)	فخذ خنزير
pâté	maʿʒūn laḥm (m)	معجون لحم
liver	kibda (f)	كبدة

mince (minced meat)	ḥaʃwa (f)	حشوة
tongue	lisān (m)	لسان
egg	bayḍa (f)	بيضة
eggs	bayḍ (m)	بيض
egg white	bayāḍ al bayḍ (m)	بياض البيض
egg yolk	ṣafār al bayḍ (m)	صفار البيض
fish	samak (m)	سمك
seafood	fawākih al baḥr (pl)	فواكه البحر
caviar	kaviyār (m)	كافيار
crab	salṭaʿūn (m)	سلطعون
prawn	ʒambari (m)	جمبري
oyster	maḥār (m)	محار
spiny lobster	karkand ʃāik (m)	كركند شائك
octopus	uxṭubūṭ (m)	أخطبوط
squid	kalmāri (m)	كالماري
sturgeon	samak al ḥaʃʃ (m)	سمك الحفش
salmon	salmūn (m)	سلمون
halibut	samak al halbūt (m)	سمك الهلبوت
cod	samak al qudd (m)	سمك القدّ
mackerel	usqumriy (m)	أسقمريّ
tuna	tūna (f)	تونة
eel	ḥankalīs (m)	حنكليس
trout	salmūn muraqqaṭ (m)	سلمون مرقّط
sardine	sardīn (m)	سردين
pike	samak al karāki (m)	سمك الكراكي
herring	rinʒa (f)	رنجة
bread	xubz (m)	خبز
cheese	ʒubna (f)	جبنة
sugar	sukkar (m)	سكّر
salt	milḥ (m)	ملح
rice	urz (m)	أرز
pasta (macaroni)	makarūna (f)	مكرونة
noodles	nūdlis (f)	نودلز
butter	zubda (f)	زبدة
vegetable oil	zayt (m)	زيت
sunflower oil	zayt ʿabīd aʃ ʃams (m)	زيت عبيد الشمس
margarine	marɣarīn (m)	مرغرين
olives	zaytūn (m)	زيتون
olive oil	zayt az zaytūn (m)	زيت الزيتون
milk	ḥalīb (m)	حليب
condensed milk	ḥalīb mukaθθaf (m)	حليب مكثف
yogurt	yūɣurt (m)	يوغورت
soured cream	krīma ḥāmiḍa (f)	كريمة حامضة
cream (of milk)	krīma (f)	كريمة
mayonnaise	mayunīz (m)	مايونيز

buttercream	krīmat zubda (f)	كريمة زبدة
groats (barley ~, etc.)	ḥubūb (pl)	حبوب
flour	daqīq (m)	دقيق
tinned food	mu'allabāt (pl)	معلبات
cornflakes	kurn fliks (m)	كورن فليكس
honey	'asal (m)	عسل
jam	murabba (m)	مربّى
chewing gum	'ilk (m)	علك

53. Drinks

water	mā' (m)	ماء
drinking water	mā' ʃurb (m)	ماء شرب
mineral water	mā' ma'daniy (m)	ماء معدني
still (adj)	bi dūn ɣāz	بدون غاز
carbonated (adj)	mukarban	مكربن
sparkling (adj)	bil ɣāz	بالغاز
ice	θalʒ (m)	ثلج
with ice	biθ θalʒ	بالثلج
non-alcoholic (adj)	bi dūn kuḥūl	بدون كحول
soft drink	maʃrūb ɣāziy (m)	مشروب غازي
refreshing drink	maʃrūb muθallaʒ (m)	مشروب مثلج
lemonade	ʃarāb laymūn (m)	شراب ليمون
spirits	maʃrūbāt kuḥūliyya (pl)	مشروبيات كحوليّة
wine	nabīð (f)	نبيذ
white wine	nibīð abyaḍ (m)	نبيذ أبيض
red wine	nabīð aḥmar (m)	نبيذ أحمر
liqueur	liqiūr (m)	ليكيور
champagne	ʃambāniya (f)	شمبانيا
vermouth	virmut (m)	فيرموث
whisky	wiski (m)	وسكي
vodka	vudka (f)	فودكا
gin	ʒīn (m)	جين
cognac	kunyāk (m)	كونياك
rum	rum (m)	رم
coffee	qahwa (f)	قهوة
black coffee	qahwa sāda (f)	قهوة سادة
white coffee	qahwa bil ḥalīb (f)	قهوة بالحليب
cappuccino	kaputʃīnu (m)	كابتشينو
instant coffee	niskafi (m)	نيسكافيه
milk	ḥalīb (m)	حليب
cocktail	kuktayl (m)	كوكتيل
milkshake	milk ʃiyk (m)	ميلك شيك
juice	'aṣīr (m)	عصير
tomato juice	'aṣīr ṭamāṭim (m)	عصير طماطم

orange juice	ʿaṣīr burtuqāl (m)	عصير برتقال
freshly squeezed juice	ʿaṣīr ṭāziʒ (m)	عصير طازج
beer	bīra (f)	بيرة
lager	bīra ḫafīfa (f)	بيرة خفيفة
bitter	bīra ɣāmiqa (f)	بيرة غامقة
tea	ʃāy (m)	شاي
black tea	ʃāy aswad (m)	شاي أسود
green tea	ʃāy aḫḍar (m)	شاي أخضر

54. Vegetables

vegetables	ḫuḍār (pl)	خضار
greens	ḫuḍrawāt waraqiyya (pl)	خضروات ورقية
tomato	ṭamāṭim (f)	طماطم
cucumber	ḫiyār (m)	خيار
carrot	ʒazar (m)	جزر
potato	baṭāṭis (f)	بطاطس
onion	baṣal (m)	بصل
garlic	θūm (m)	ثوم
cabbage	kurumb (m)	كرنب
cauliflower	qarnabīṭ (m)	قرنبيط
Brussels sprouts	kurumb brūksil (m)	كرنب بروكسل
broccoli	brukuli (m)	بركولي
beetroot	banʒar (m)	بنجر
aubergine	bātinʒān (m)	باذنجان
courgette	kūsa (f)	كوسة
pumpkin	qarʿ (m)	قرع
turnip	lift (m)	لفت
parsley	baqdūnis (m)	بقدونس
dill	ʃabat (m)	شبت
lettuce	ḫass (m)	خسّ
celery	karafs (m)	كرفس
asparagus	halyūn (m)	هليون
spinach	sabāniḫ (m)	سبانخ
pea	bisilla (f)	بسلّة
beans	fūl (m)	فول
maize	ðura (f)	ذرّة
kidney bean	faṣūliya (f)	فاصوليا
sweet paper	filfil (m)	فلفل
radish	fiʒl (m)	فجل
artichoke	ḫurʃūf (m)	خرشوف

55. Fruits. Nuts

| fruit | fākiha (f) | فاكهة |
| apple | tuffāḥa (f) | تفّاحة |

pear	kummaθra (f)	كمثرى
lemon	laymūn (m)	ليمون
orange	burtuqāl (m)	برتقال
strawberry (garden ~)	farawla (f)	فراولة
tangerine	yūsufiy (m)	يوسفي
plum	barqūq (m)	برقوق
peach	durrāq (m)	دراق
apricot	miʃmiʃ (f)	مشمش
raspberry	tūt al ʿullayq al aḥmar (m)	توت العليق الأحمر
pineapple	ananās (m)	أناناس
banana	mawz (m)	موز
watermelon	baṭṭīχ aḥmar (m)	بطيخ أحمر
grape	ʿinab (m)	عنب
cherry	karaz (m)	كرز
melon	baṭṭīχ aṣfar (f)	بطيخ أصفر
grapefruit	zinbāʿ (m)	زنباع
avocado	avukādu (f)	افوكاتو
papaya	babāya (m)	بابايا
mango	mangu (m)	مانجو
pomegranate	rummān (m)	رمان
redcurrant	kiʃmiʃ aḥmar (m)	كشمش أحمر
blackcurrant	ʿinab aθ θaʿlab al aswad (m)	عنب الثعلب الأسود
gooseberry	ʿinab aθ θaʿlab (m)	عنب الثعلب
bilberry	ʿinab al aḥrāʒ (m)	عنب الأحراج
blackberry	θamar al ʿullayk (m)	ثمر العليّق
raisin	zabīb (m)	زبيب
fig	tīn (m)	تين
date	tamr (m)	تمر
peanut	fūl sudāniy (m)	فول سودانيّ
almond	lawz (m)	لوز
walnut	ʿayn al ʒamal (f)	عين الجمل
hazelnut	bunduq (m)	بندق
coconut	ʒawz al hind (m)	جوز هند
pistachios	fustuq (m)	فستق

56. Bread. Sweets

bakers' confectionery (pastry)	ḥalawiyyāt (pl)	حلويّات
bread	χubz (m)	خبز
biscuits	baskawīt (m)	بسكويت
chocolate (n)	ʃukulāta (f)	شكولاتة
chocolate (as adj)	biʃ ʃukulāṭa	بالشكولاتة
candy (wrapped)	bumbūn (m)	بونبون
cake (e.g. cupcake)	kaʿk (m)	كعك
cake (e.g. birthday ~)	tūrta (f)	تورتة
pie (e.g. apple ~)	faṭīra (f)	فطيرة
filling (for cake, pie)	ḥaʃwa (f)	حشوة

jam (whole fruit jam)	murabba (m)	مربّى
marmalade	marmalād (f)	مرملاد
wafers	wāfil (m)	وافل
ice-cream	muθallaʒāt (pl)	مثلجات
pudding (Christmas ~)	būding (m)	بودنج

57. Spices

salt	milḥ (m)	ملح
salty (adj)	māliḥ	مالح
to salt (vt)	mallaḥ	ملح
black pepper	filfil aswad (m)	فلفل أسود
red pepper (milled ~)	filfil aḥmar (m)	فلفل أحمر
mustard	ṣalṣat al χardal (f)	صلصة الخردل
horseradish	fiʒl ḥārr (m)	فجل حارّ
condiment	tābil (m)	تابل
spice	bahār (m)	بهار
sauce	ṣalṣa (f)	صلصة
vinegar	χall (m)	خلّ
anise	yānsūn (m)	يانسون
basil	rīḥān (m)	ريحان
cloves	qurumful (m)	قرنفل
ginger	zanʒabīl (m)	زنجبيل
coriander	kuzbara (f)	كزبرة
cinnamon	qirfa (f)	قرفة
sesame	simsim (m)	سمسم
bay leaf	awrāq al χār (pl)	أوراق الغار
paprika	babrika (f)	بابريكا
caraway	karāwiya (f)	كراوية
saffron	za'farān (m)	زعفران

PERSONAL INFORMATION. FAMILY

58. Personal information. Forms

name (first name)	ism (m)	إسم
surname (last name)	ism al 'ā'ila (m)	إسم العائلة
date of birth	tarīχ al mīlād (m)	تاريخ الميلاد
place of birth	makān al mīlād (m)	مكان الميلاد
nationality	ʒinsiyya (f)	جنسية
place of residence	maqarr al iqāma (m)	مقر الإقامة
country	balad (m)	بلد
profession (occupation)	mihna (f)	مهنة
gender, sex	ʒins (m)	جنس
height	ṭūl (m)	طول
weight	wazn (m)	وزن

59. Family members. Relatives

mother	umm (f)	أُمّ
father	ab (m)	أب
son	ibn (m)	إبن
daughter	ibna (f)	إبنة
younger daughter	al ibna aṣ ṣaɣīra (f)	الإبنة الصغيرة
younger son	al ibn aṣ ṣaɣīr (m)	الابن الصغير
eldest daughter	al ibna al kabīra (f)	الإبنة الكبيرة
eldest son	al ibn al kabīr (m)	الإبن الكبير
brother	aχ (m)	أخ
elder brother	al aχ al kabīr (m)	الأخ الكبير
younger brother	al aχ aṣ ṣaɣīr (m)	الأخ الصغير
sister	uχt (f)	أخت
elder sister	al uχt al kabīra (f)	الأخت الكبيرة
younger sister	al uχt aṣ ṣaɣīra (f)	الأخت الصغيرة
cousin (masc.)	ibn 'amm (m), ibn χāl (m)	إبن عمّ، إبن خال
cousin (fem.)	ibnat 'amm (f), ibnat χāl (f)	إبنة عم، إبنة خال
mummy	mama (f)	ماما
dad, daddy	baba (m)	بابا
parents	wālidān (du)	والدان
child	ṭifl (m)	طفل
children	aṭfāl (pl)	أطفال
grandmother	ʒidda (f)	جدّة
grandfather	ʒadd (m)	جدّ
grandson	ḥafīd (m)	حفيد

| granddaughter | ḥafīda (f) | حفيدة |
| grandchildren | aḥfād (pl) | أحفاد |

uncle	'amm (m), χāl (m)	عمّ, خال
aunt	'amma (f), χāla (f)	عمّة, خالة
nephew	ibn al aχ (m), ibn al uχt (m)	إبن الأخ, إبن الأخت
niece	ibnat al aχ (f), ibnat al uχt (f)	إبنة الأخ, إبنة الأخت
mother-in-law (wife's mother)	ḥamātt (f)	حماة
father-in-law (husband's father)	ḥamm (m)	حم
son-in-law (daughter's husband)	zaw3 al ibna (m)	زوج الأبنة
stepmother	zaw3at al ab (f)	زوجة الأب
stepfather	zaw3 al umm (m)	زوج الأمّ

infant	ṭifl raḍī' (m)	طفل رضيع
baby (infant)	mawlūd (m)	مولود
little boy, kid	walad ṣaɣīr (m)	ولد صغير

wife	zaw3a (f)	زوجة
husband	zaw3 (m)	زوج
spouse (husband)	zaw3 (m)	زوج
spouse (wife)	zaw3a (f)	زوجة

married (masc.)	mutazawwi3	متزوِّج
married (fem.)	mutazawwi3a	متزوِّجة
single (unmarried)	a'zab	أعزب
bachelor	a'zab (m)	أعزب
divorced (masc.)	muṭallaq (m)	مطلَّق
widow	armala (f)	أرملة
widower	armal (m)	أرمل

relative	qarīb (m)	قريب
close relative	nasīb qarīb (m)	نسيب قريب
distant relative	nasīb ba'īd (m)	نسيب بعيد
relatives	aqārib (pl)	أقارب

orphan (boy or girl)	yatīm (m)	يتيم
guardian (of a minor)	waliyy amr (m)	ولي أمر
to adopt (a boy)	tabanna	تبنّى
to adopt (a girl)	tabanna	تبنّى

60. Friends. Colleagues

friend (masc.)	ṣadīq (m)	صديق
friend (fem.)	ṣadīqa (f)	صديقة
friendship	ṣadāqa (f)	صداقة
to be friends	ṣādaq	صادق

pal (masc.)	ṣāḥib (m)	صاحب
pal (fem.)	ṣaḥiba (f)	صاحبة
partner	rafīq (m)	رفيق
chief (boss)	ra'īs (m)	رئيس

superior (n)	ra'īs (m)	رئيس
owner, proprietor	ṣāḥib (m)	صاحب
subordinate (n)	tābi' (m)	تابع
colleague	zamīl (m)	زميل

acquaintance (person)	ma'ruf (m)	معروف
fellow traveller	rafīq safar (m)	رفيق سفر
classmate	zamīl fiṣ ṣaff (m)	زميل في الصفّ

neighbour (masc.)	ʒār (m)	جار
neighbour (fem.)	ʒāra (f)	جارة
neighbours	ʒirān (pl)	جيران

HUMAN BODY. MEDICINE

61. Head

head	ra's (m)	رأس
face	waʒh (m)	وجه
nose	anf (m)	أنف
mouth	fam (m)	فم
eye	ʿayn (f)	عين
eyes	ʿuyūn (pl)	عيون
pupil	ḥadaqa (f)	حدقة
eyebrow	ḥāʒib (m)	حاجب
eyelash	rimʃ (m)	رمش
eyelid	ʒafn (m)	جفن
tongue	lisān (m)	لسان
tooth	sinn (f)	سِنّ
lips	ʃifāh (pl)	شفاه
cheekbones	ʿiẓām waʒhiyya (pl)	عظام وجهيّة
gum	liθθa (f)	لِثّة
palate	ḥanak (m)	حنك
nostrils	minχarān (du)	منخران
chin	ðaqan (m)	ذقن
jaw	fakk (m)	فكّ
cheek	χadd (m)	خدّ
forehead	ʒabha (f)	جبهة
temple	ṣudɣ (m)	صدغ
ear	uðun (f)	أذن
back of the head	qafa (m)	قفا
neck	raqaba (f)	رقبة
throat	ḥalq (m)	حلق
hair	ʃaʿr (m)	شعر
hairstyle	tasrīḥa (f)	تسريحة
haircut	tasrīḥa (f)	تسريحة
wig	barūka (f)	باروكة
moustache	ʃawārib (pl)	شوارب
beard	liḥya (f)	لحية
to have (a beard, etc.)	ʿindahu	عنده
plait	ḍifīra (f)	ضفيرة
sideboards	sawālif (pl)	سوالف
red-haired (adj)	aḥmar aʃ ʃaʿr	أحمر الشعر
grey (hair)	abyaḍ	أبيض
bald (adj)	aṣlaʿ	أصلع
bald patch	ṣalaʿ (m)	صلع

| ponytail | ðayl ḥiṣān (m) | ذيل حصان |
| fringe | quṣṣa (f) | قصّة |

62. Human body

| hand | yad (m) | يد |
| arm | ðirāʿ (f) | ذراع |

finger	iṣbaʿ (m)	إصبع
toe	iṣbaʿ al qadam (m)	إصبع القدم
thumb	ibhām (m)	إبهام
little finger	χunṣur (m)	خنصر
nail	ẓufr (m)	ظفر

fist	qabḍa (f)	قبضة
palm	kaff (f)	كفّ
wrist	miʿṣam (m)	معصم
forearm	sāʿid (m)	ساعد
elbow	mirfaq (m)	مرفق
shoulder	katf (f)	كتف

leg	riʒl (f)	رجل
foot	qadam (f)	قدم
knee	rukba (f)	ركبة
calf	sammāna (f)	سمّانة
hip	faχð (f)	فخذ
heel	ʿaqb (m)	عقب

body	ʒism (m)	جسم
stomach	baṭn (m)	بطن
chest	ṣadr (m)	صدر
breast	θady (m)	ثدي
flank	ʒamb (m)	جنب
back	ẓahr (m)	ظهر
lower back	asfal aẓ ẓahr (m)	أسفل الظهر
waist	χaṣr (m)	خصر

navel (belly button)	surra (f)	سرّة
buttocks	ardāf (pl)	أرداف
bottom	dubr (m)	دبر

beauty spot	ʃāma (f)	شامة
birthmark (café au lait spot)	waḥma	وحمة
tattoo	waʃm (m)	وشم
scar	nadba (f)	ندبة

63. Diseases

illness	maraḍ (m)	مرض
to be ill	maraḍ	مرض
health	ṣiḥḥa (f)	صحّة
runny nose (coryza)	zukām (m)	زكام

tonsillitis	iltihāb al lawzatayn (m)	التهاب اللوزتين
cold (illness)	bard (m)	برد
to catch a cold	aṣābahu al bard	أصابه البرد
bronchitis	iltihāb al qaṣabāt (m)	إلتهاب القصبات
pneumonia	iltihāb ar ri'atayn (m)	إلتهاب الرئتين
flu, influenza	inflūnza (f)	إنفلونزا
shortsighted (adj)	qaṣīr an naẓar	قصير النظر
longsighted (adj)	ba'īd an naẓar	بعيد النظر
strabismus (crossed eyes)	ḥawal (m)	حول
squint-eyed (adj)	aḥwal	أحول
cataract	katarakt (f)	كاتاراكت
glaucoma	glawkūma (f)	جلوكوما
stroke	sakta (f)	سكتة
heart attack	iḥtifā' (m)	إحتشاء
myocardial infarction	nawba qalbiya (f)	نوبة قلبية
paralysis	ʃalal (m)	شلل
to paralyse (vt)	ʃall	شلّ
allergy	ḥassāsiyya (f)	حسّاسيّة
asthma	rabw (m)	ربو
diabetes	ad dā' as sukkariy (m)	الداء السكّريّ
toothache	alam al asnān (m)	ألم الأسنان
caries	naxar al asnān (m)	نخر الأسنان
diarrhoea	ishāl (m)	إسهال
constipation	imsāk (m)	إمساك
stomach upset	'usr al haḍm (m)	عسر الهضم
food poisoning	tasammum (m)	تسمّم
to get food poisoning	tasammam	تسمّم
arthritis	iltihāb al mafāṣil (m)	إلتهاب المفاصل
rickets	kusāḥ al aṭfāl (m)	كساح الأطفال
rheumatism	riumatizm (m)	روماتزم
atherosclerosis	taṣṣallub aʃ ʃarayīn (m)	تصلّب الشرايين
gastritis	iltihāb al ma'ida (m)	إلتهاب المعدة
appendicitis	iltihāb az zā'ida ad dūdiyya (m)	إلتهاب الزائدة الدوديّة
cholecystitis	iltihāb al marāra (m)	إلتهاب المرارة
ulcer	qurḥa (f)	قرحة
measles	maraḍ al ḥaṣba (m)	مرض الحصبة
rubella (German measles)	ḥaṣba almāniyya (f)	حصبة ألمانية
jaundice	yaraqān (m)	يرقان
hepatitis	iltihāb al kabd al vayrūsiy (m)	إلتهاب الكبد الفيروسيّ
schizophrenia	ʃizufrīniya (f)	شيزوفرينيا
rabies (hydrophobia)	dā' al kalb (m)	داء الكلب
neurosis	'iṣāb (m)	عصاب
concussion	irtiʒāʒ al muxx (m)	إرتجاج المخ
cancer	saraṭān (m)	سرطان
sclerosis	taṣṣallub (m)	تصلّب

multiple sclerosis	taṣṣallub mutaʻaddid (m)	تصلّب متعدد
alcoholism	idmān al χamr (m)	إدمان الخمر
alcoholic (n)	mudmin al χamr (m)	مدمن الخمر
syphilis	sifilis az zuhariy (m)	سفلس الزهري
AIDS	al aydz (m)	الايدز

tumour	waram (m)	ورم
malignant (adj)	χabīθ	خبيث
benign (adj)	ḥamīd (m)	حميد

fever	ḥumma (f)	حمّى
malaria	malāriya (f)	ملاريا
gangrene	ɣanɣrīna (f)	غنغرينا
seasickness	duwār al baḥr (m)	دوار البحر
epilepsy	maraḍ aṣ ṣarʻ (m)	مرض الصرع

epidemic	wabāʼ (m)	وباء
typhus	tīfus (m)	تيفوس
tuberculosis	maraḍ as sull (m)	مرض السلّ
cholera	kulīra (f)	كوليرا
plague (bubonic ~)	ṭāʻūn (m)	طاعون

64. Symptoms. Treatments. Part 1

symptom	ʻaraḍ (m)	عرض
temperature	ḥarāra (f)	حرارة
high temperature (fever)	ḥumma (f)	حمّى
pulse (heartbeat)	nabḍ (m)	نبض

dizziness (vertigo)	dawχa (f)	دوخة
hot (adj)	ḥārr	حارّ
shivering	nafaḍān (m)	نفضان
pale (e.g. ~ face)	aṣfar	أصفر

cough	suʻāl (m)	سعال
to cough (vi)	saʻal	سعل
to sneeze (vi)	ʻaṭas	عطس
faint	iɣmāʼ (m)	إغماء
to faint (vi)	ɣumiya ʻalayh	غمي عليه

bruise (hématome)	kadma (f)	كدمة
bump (lump)	tawarrum (m)	تورّم
to bang (bump)	iṣṭadam	إصطدم
contusion (bruise)	raḍḍ (m)	رضّ
to get a bruise	taraḍḍaḍ	ترضّض

to limp (vi)	ʻaraʒ	عرج
dislocation	χalʻ (m)	خلع
to dislocate (vt)	χalaʻ	خلع
fracture	kasr (m)	كسر
to have a fracture	inkasar	إنكسر

cut (e.g. paper ~)	ʒurḥ (m)	جرح
to cut oneself	ʒaraḥ nafsah	جرح نفسه

bleeding	nazf (m)	نزف
burn (injury)	ḥarq (m)	حرق
to get burned	taʃayyat	تشيّط
to prick (vt)	waχaz	وخز
to prick oneself	waχaz nafsah	وخز نفسه
to injure (vt)	aṣāb	أصاب
injury	iṣāba (f)	إصابة
wound	ʒurḥ (m)	جرح
trauma	ṣadma (f)	صدمة
to be delirious	haða	هذى
to stutter (vi)	talaʿsam	تلعثم
sunstroke	ḍarbat ʃams (f)	ضربة شمس

65. Symptoms. Treatments. Part 2

pain, ache	alam (m)	ألم
splinter (in foot, etc.)	ʃaẓiyya (f)	شظيّة
sweat (perspiration)	ʿirq (m)	عرق
to sweat (perspire)	ʿariq	عرق
vomiting	taqayyuʿ (m)	تقيّؤ
convulsions	taʃannuʒāt (pl)	تشنّجات
pregnant (adj)	ḥāmil	حامل
to be born	wulid	وُلد
delivery, labour	wilāda (f)	ولادة
to deliver (~ a baby)	walad	ولد
abortion	iʒhāḍ (m)	إجهاض
breathing, respiration	tanaffus (m)	تنفّس
in-breath (inhalation)	istinʃāq (m)	إستنشاق
out-breath (exhalation)	zafīr (m)	زفير
to exhale (breathe out)	zafar	زفر
to inhale (vi)	istanʃaq	إستنشق
disabled person	muʿāq (m)	معاق
cripple	muqʿad (m)	مقعد
drug addict	mudmin muχaddirāt (m)	مدمن مخدّرات
deaf (adj)	aṭraʃ	أطرش
mute (adj)	aχras	أخرس
deaf mute (adj)	aṭraʃ aχras	أطرش أخرس
mad, insane (adj)	maʒnūn	مجنون
madman	maʒnūn (m)	مجنون
(demented person)		
madwoman	maʒnūna (f)	مجنونة
to go insane	ʒunn	جُنّ
gene	ʒīn (m)	جين
immunity	manāʿa (f)	مناعة
hereditary (adj)	wirāθiy	وراثيّ

congenital (adj)	xilqiy munð al wilāda	خلقيّ منذ الولادة
virus	virūs (m)	فيروس
microbe	mikrūb (m)	ميكروب
bacterium	ʒurθūma (f)	جرثومة
infection	ʿadwa (f)	عدوى

66. Symptoms. Treatments. Part 3

hospital	mustaʃfa (m)	مستشفى
patient	marīḍ (m)	مريض
diagnosis	taʃxīṣ (m)	تشخيص
cure	ʿilāʒ (m)	علاج
medical treatment	ʿilāʒ (m)	علاج
to get treatment	taʿālaʒ	تعالج
to treat (~ a patient)	ʿālaʒ	عالج
to nurse (look after)	marraḍ	مرّض
care (nursing ~)	ʿināya (f)	عناية
operation, surgery	ʿamaliyya ʒarahiyya (f)	عمليّة جرحيّة
to bandage (head, limb)	ḍammad	ضمّد
bandaging	taḍmīd (m)	تضميد
vaccination	talqīḥ (m)	تلقيح
to vaccinate (vt)	laqqaḥ	لقّح
injection	ḥuqna (f)	حقنة
to give an injection	ḥaqan ibra	حقن إبرة
attack	nawba (f)	نوبة
amputation	batr (m)	بتر
to amputate (vt)	batar	بتر
coma	ɣaybūba (f)	غبوبة
to be in a coma	kān fi ḥālat ɣaybūba	كان في حالة غبوبة
intensive care	al ʿināya al murakkaza (f)	العناية المركّزة
to recover (~ from flu)	ʃufiy	شفي
condition (patient's ~)	ḥāla (f)	حالة
consciousness	waʿy (m)	وعي
memory (faculty)	ðākira (f)	ذاكرة
to pull out (tooth)	xalaʿ	خلع
filling	ḥaʃw (m)	حشو
to fill (a tooth)	ḥaʃa	حشا
hypnosis	at tanwīm al maɣnaṭīsiy (m)	التنويم المغناطيسيّ
to hypnotize (vt)	nawwam	نوّم

67. Medicine. Drugs. Accessories

medicine, drug	dawā' (m)	دواء
remedy	ʿilāʒ (m)	علاج
to prescribe (vt)	waṣaf	وصف

prescription	waṣfa (f)	وصفة
tablet, pill	qurṣ (m)	قرص
ointment	marham (m)	مرهم
ampoule	ambūla (f)	أمبولة
mixture, solution	dawā' ʃarāb (m)	دواء شراب
syrup	ʃarāb (m)	شراب
capsule	ḥabba (f)	حبّة
powder	ðarūr (m)	ذرور

gauze bandage	ḍammāda (f)	ضمادة
cotton wool	quṭn (m)	قطن
iodine	yūd (m)	يود

plaster	blāstir (m)	بلاستر
eyedropper	māṣṣat al bastara (f)	ماصّة البسترة
thermometer	tirmūmitr (m)	ترمومتر
syringe	miḥqana (f)	محقنة

| wheelchair | kursiy mutaḥarrik (m) | كرسي متحرّك |
| crutches | 'ukkāzān (du) | عكّازان |

painkiller	musakkin (m)	مسكّن
laxative	mulayyin (m)	ملّين
spirits (ethanol)	iθanūl (m)	إيثانول
medicinal herbs	a'ʃāb ṭibbiyya (pl)	أعشاب طبية
herbal (~ tea)	'uʃbiy	عشبي

FLAT

68. Flat

flat	ʃaqqa (f)	شقّة
room	ɣurfa (f)	غرفة
bedroom	ɣurfat an nawm (f)	غرفة النوم
dining room	ɣurfat il akl (f)	غرفة الأكل
living room	ṣālat al istiqbāl (f)	صالة الإستقبال
study (home office)	maktab (m)	مكتب
entry room	madχal (m)	مدخل
bathroom	ḥammām (m)	حمّام
water closet	ḥammām (m)	حمّام
ceiling	saqf (m)	سقف
floor	arḍ (f)	أرض
corner	zāwiya (f)	زاوية

69. Furniture. Interior

furniture	aθāθ (m)	أثاث
table	maktab (m)	مكتب
chair	kursiy (m)	كرسيّ
bed	sarīr (m)	سرير
sofa, settee	kanaba (f)	كنبة
armchair	kursiy (m)	كرسيّ
bookcase	χizānat kutub (f)	خزانة كتب
shelf	raff (m)	رفّ
wardrobe	dūlāb (m)	دولاب
coat rack (wall-mounted ~)	ʃammāʿa (f)	شمّاعة
coat stand	ʃammāʿa (f)	شمّاعة
chest of drawers	dulāb adrāʒ (m)	دولاب أدراج
coffee table	ṭāwilat al qahwa (f)	طاولة القهوة
mirror	mir'āt (f)	مرآة
carpet	siʒāda (f)	سجادة
small carpet	siʒāda (f)	سجادة
fireplace	midfa'a ḥā'iṭiyya (f)	مدفأة حائطيّة
candle	ʃamʿa (f)	شمعة
candlestick	ʃamʿadān (m)	شمعدان
drapes	satā'ir (pl)	ستائر
wallpaper	waraq ḥīṭān (m)	ورق حيطان

blinds (jalousie)	haṣīrat ʃubbāk (f)	حصيرة شبّاك
table lamp	miṣbāḥ aṭ ṭāwila (m)	مصباح الطاولة
wall lamp (sconce)	miṣbāḥ al ḥāʾiṭ (f)	مصباح الحائط
standard lamp	miṣbāḥ arḍiy (m)	مصباح أرضيّ
chandelier	naʒafa (f)	نجفة

leg (of a chair, table)	riʒl (f)	رجل
armrest	masnad (m)	مسند
back (backrest)	masnad (m)	مسند
drawer	durʒ (m)	درج

70. Bedding

bedclothes	bayāḍāt as sarīr (pl)	بياضات السرير
pillow	wisāda (f)	وسادة
pillowslip	kīs al wisāda (m)	كيس الوسادة
duvet	baṭṭāniyya (f)	بطّانيّة
sheet	milāya (f)	ملاية
bedspread	ɣiṭāʾ as sarīr (m)	غطاء السرير

71. Kitchen

kitchen	maṭbaχ (m)	مطبخ
gas	ɣāz (m)	غاز
gas cooker	butuɣāz (m)	بوتوغاز
electric cooker	furn kaharabāʾiy (m)	فرن كهربائيّ
oven	furn (m)	فرن
microwave oven	furn al mikruwayv (m)	فرن الميكروويف

refrigerator	θallāʒa (f)	ثلاجة
freezer	frīzir (m)	فريزر
dishwasher	ɣassāla (f)	غسّالة

mincer	farrāmat laḥm (f)	فرّامة لحم
juicer	ʿaṣṣāra (f)	عصّارة
toaster	maḥmaṣat χubz (f)	محمصة خبز
mixer	χallāṭ (m)	خلّاط

coffee machine	mākinat ṣanʿ al qahwa (f)	ماكينة صنع القهوة
coffee pot	kanaka (f)	كنكة
coffee grinder	maṭḥanat qahwa (f)	مطحنة قهوة

kettle	barrād (m)	برّاد
teapot	barrād aʃʃāy (m)	برّاد الشاي
lid	ɣiṭāʾ (m)	غطاء
tea strainer	miṣfāt (f)	مصفاة

spoon	milʿaqa (f)	ملعقة
teaspoon	milʿaqat ʃāy (f)	ملعقة شاي
soup spoon	milʿaqa kabīra (f)	ملعقة كبيرة
fork	ʃawka (f)	شوكة
knife	sikkīn (m)	سكّين

tableware (dishes)	ṣuḥūn (pl)	صحون
plate (dinner ~)	ṭabaq (m)	طبق
saucer	ṭabaq finʒān (m)	طبق فنجان

shot glass	ka's (f)	كأس
glass (tumbler)	kubbāya (f)	كبّاية
cup	finʒān (m)	فنجان

sugar bowl	sukkariyya (f)	سكّرِيَّة
salt cellar	mamlaḥa (f)	مملحة
pepper pot	mabhara (f)	مبهرة
butter dish	ṣuḥn zubda (m)	صحن زبدة

stock pot (soup pot)	kassirūlla (f)	كاسرولة
frying pan (skillet)	ṭāsa (f)	طاسة
ladle	miɣrafa (f)	مغرفة
colander	miṣfāt (f)	مصفاة
tray (serving ~)	ṣīniyya (f)	صينيّة

bottle	zuʒāʒa (f)	زجاجة
jar (glass)	barṭamān (m)	برطمان
tin (can)	tanaka (f)	تنكة

bottle opener	fattāḥa (f)	فتّاحة
tin opener	fattāḥa (f)	فتّاحة
corkscrew	barrīma (f)	برِيمة
filter	filtir (m)	فلتر
to filter (vt)	ṣaffa	صفّى

| waste (food ~, etc.) | zubāla (f) | زبالة |
| waste bin (kitchen ~) | ṣundūq az zubāla (m) | صندوق الزبالة |

72. Bathroom

bathroom	ḥammām (m)	حمّام
water	mā' (m)	ماء
tap	ḥanafiyya (f)	حنفيّة
hot water	mā' sāχin (m)	ماء ساخن
cold water	mā' bārid (m)	ماء بارد

toothpaste	ma'ʒūn asnān (m)	معجون أسنان
to clean one's teeth	naẓẓaf al asnān	نظف الأسنان
toothbrush	furʃat asnān (f)	فرشة أسنان

to shave (vi)	ḥalaq	حلق
shaving foam	raɣwa lil ḥilāqa (f)	رغوة للحلاقة
razor	mūs ḥilāqa (m)	موس حلاقة

to wash (one's hands, etc.)	ɣasal	غسل
to have a bath	istaḥamm	إستحمّ
shower	dūʃ (m)	دوش
to have a shower	aχað ad duʃ	أخذ الدش
bath	ḥawḍ istiḥmām (m)	حوض استحمام
toilet (toilet bowl)	mirḥāḍ (m)	مرحاض

sink (washbasin)	ḥawḍ (m)	حوض
soap	ṣābūn (m)	صابون
soap dish	ṣabbāna (f)	صبّانة
sponge	līfa (f)	ليفة
shampoo	ʃāmbū (m)	شامبو
towel	fūṭa (f)	فوطة
bathrobe	θawb ḥammām (m)	ثوب حمّام
laundry (laundering)	ɣasīl (m)	غسيل
washing machine	ɣassāla (f)	غسّالة
to do the laundry	ɣasal al malābis	غسل الملابس
washing powder	masḥūq ɣasīl (m)	مسحوق غسيل

73. Household appliances

TV, telly	tilivizyūn (m)	تليفزيون
tape recorder	ʒihāz tasʒīl (m)	جهاز تسجيل
video	ʒihāz tasʒīl vidiyu (m)	جهاز تسجيل فيديو
radio	ʒihāz radiyu (m)	جهاز راديو
player (CD, MP3, etc.)	blayir (m)	بلاير
video projector	ʿāriḍ vidiyu (m)	عارض فيديو
home cinema	sinima manziliyya (f)	سينما منزليّة
DVD player	di vi di (m)	دي في دي
amplifier	mukabbir aṣ ṣawt (m)	مكبّر الصوت
video game console	ʾatāri (m)	أتاري
video camera	kamira vidiyu (f)	كاميرا فيديو
camera (photo)	kamira (f)	كاميرا
digital camera	kamira diʒital (f)	كاميرا ديجيتال
vacuum cleaner	miknasa kahrabāʾiyya (f)	مكنسة كهربائيّة
iron (e.g. steam ~)	makwāt (f)	مكواة
ironing board	lawḥat kayy (f)	لوحة كيّ
telephone	hātif (m)	هاتف
mobile phone	hātif maḥmūl (m)	هاتف محمول
typewriter	ʾāla katiba (f)	آلة كاتبة
sewing machine	ʾālat χiyāṭa (f)	آلة الخياطة
microphone	mikrufūn (m)	ميكروفون
headphones	sammāʿāt raʾsiya (pl)	سمّاعات رأسيّة
remote control (TV)	rimuwt kuntrūl (m)	ريموت كنترول
CD, compact disc	si di (m)	سي دي
cassette, tape	ʃarīṭ (m)	شريط
vinyl record	usṭuwāna (f)	أسطوانة

THE EARTH. WEATHER

74. Outer space

space	faḍā' (m)	فضاء
space (as adj)	faḍā'iy	فضائيّ
outer space	faḍā' (m)	فضاء
world	'ālam (m)	عالم
universe	al kawn (m)	الكون
galaxy	al maʒarra (f)	المجرّة
star	naʒm (m)	نجم
constellation	burʒ (m)	برج
planet	kawkab (m)	كوكب
satellite	qamar ṣinā'iy (m)	قمر صناعيّ
meteorite	ḥaʒar nayzakiy (m)	حجر نيزكيّ
comet	muðannab (m)	مذنّب
asteroid	kuwaykib (m)	كويكب
orbit	madār (m)	مدار
to revolve	dār	دار
(~ around the Earth)		
atmosphere	al ɣilāf al ʒawwiy (m)	الغلاف الجوّيّ
the Sun	aʃ ʃams (f)	الشمس
solar system	al maʒmū'a aʃ ʃamsiyya (f)	المجموعة الشمسيّة
solar eclipse	kusūf aʃ ʃams (m)	كسوف الشمس
the Earth	al arḍ (f)	الأرض
the Moon	al qamar (m)	القمر
Mars	al mirrīχ (m)	المرّيخ
Venus	az zahra (f)	الزهرة
Jupiter	al muʃtari (m)	المشتري
Saturn	zuḥal (m)	زحل
Mercury	'aṭārid (m)	عطارد
Uranus	urānus (m)	اورانوس
Neptune	nibtūn (m)	نبتون
Pluto	blūtu (m)	بلوتو
Milky Way	darb at tabbāna (m)	درب التبّانة
Great Bear (Ursa Major)	ad dubb al akbar (m)	الدبّ الأكبر
North Star	naʒm al 'qutb (m)	نجم القطب
Martian	sākin al mirrīχ (m)	ساكن المرّيخ
extraterrestrial (n)	faḍā'iy (m)	فضائيّ
alien	faḍā'iy (m)	فضائيّ

flying saucer	ṭabaq ṭāʾir (m)	طبق طائر
spaceship	markaba faḍāʾiyya (f)	مركبة فضائية
space station	maḥaṭṭat faḍāʾ (f)	محطة فضاء
blast-off	intilāq (m)	إنطلاق

engine	mutūr (m)	موتور
nozzle	manfaθ (m)	منفث
fuel	wuqūd (m)	وقود

| cockpit, flight deck | kabīna (f) | كابينة |
| aerial | hawāʾiy (m) | هوائيّ |

porthole	kuwwa mustadīra (f)	كوّة مستديرة
solar panel	lawḥ ʃamsiy (m)	لوح شمسيّ
spacesuit	baðlat al faḍāʾ (f)	بذلة الفضاء

| weightlessness | inʿidām al wazn (m) | إنعدام الوزن |
| oxygen | uksiʒīn (m) | أكسجين |

| docking (in space) | rasw (m) | رسو |
| to dock (vi, vt) | rasa | رسا |

| observatory | marṣad (m) | مرصد |
| telescope | tiliskūp (m) | تلسكوب |

| to observe (vt) | rāqab | راقب |
| to explore (vt) | istakʃaf | إستكشف |

75. The Earth

the Earth	al arḍ (f)	الأرض
the globe (the Earth)	al kura al arḍiyya (f)	الكرة الأرضية
planet	kawkab (m)	كوكب

atmosphere	al ɣilāf al ʒawwiy (m)	الغلاف الجوّيّ
geography	ʒuɣrāfiya (f)	جغرافيا
nature	ṭabīʿa (f)	طبيعة

globe (table ~)	namūðaʒ lil kura al arḍiyya (m)	نموذج للكرة الأرضية
map	xarīṭa (f)	خريطة
atlas	aṭlas (m)	أطلس

| Europe | urūbba (f) | أوروبّا |
| Asia | ʾāsiya (f) | آسيا |

| Africa | afrīqiya (f) | أفريقيا |
| Australia | usturāliya (f) | أستراليا |

America	amrīka (f)	أمريكا
North America	amrīka aʃ ʃimāliyya (f)	أمريكا الشمالية
South America	amrīka al ʒanūbiyya (f)	أمريكا الجنوبية

| Antarctica | al quṭb al ʒanūbiy (m) | القطب الجنوبيّ |
| the Arctic | al quṭb aʃ ʃimāliy (m) | القطب الشماليّ |

76. Cardinal directions

north	ʃimāl (m)	شمال
to the north	ilaʃ ʃimāl	إلى الشمال
in the north	fiʃ ʃimāl	في الشمال
northern (adj)	ʃimāliy	شماليّ

south	ʒanūb (m)	جنوب
to the south	ilal ʒanūb	إلى الجنوب
in the south	fil ʒanūb	في الجنوب
southern (adj)	ʒanūbiy	جنوبيّ

west	ɣarb (m)	غرب
to the west	ilal ɣarb	إلى الغرب
in the west	fil ɣarb	في الغرب
western (adj)	ɣarbiy	غربيّ

east	ʃarq (m)	شرق
to the east	ilaʃ ʃarq	إلى الشرق
in the east	fiʃ ʃarq	في الشرق
eastern (adj)	ʃarqiy	شرقيّ

77. Sea. Ocean

sea	baḥr (m)	بحر
ocean	muḥīṭ (m)	محيط
gulf (bay)	xalīʒ (m)	خليج
straits	maḍīq (m)	مضيق

land (solid ground)	barr (m)	برّ
continent (mainland)	qārra (f)	قارّة
island	ʒazīra (f)	جزيرة
peninsula	ʃibh ʒazīra (f)	شبه جزيرة
archipelago	maʒmūʿat ʒuzur (f)	مجموعة جزر

bay, cove	xalīʒ (m)	خليج
harbour	mīnā' (m)	ميناء
lagoon	buḥayra ʃāṭi'a (f)	بحيرة شاطئة
cape	ra's (m)	رأس

atoll	ʒazīra marʒāniyya istiwā'iyya (f)	جزيرة مرجانيّة إستوائيّة
reef	ʃi'āb (pl)	شعاب
coral	murʒān (m)	مرجان
coral reef	ʃi'āb marʒāniyya (pl)	شعاب مرجانيّة

deep (adj)	ʿamīq	عميق
depth (deep water)	ʿumq (m)	عمق
abyss	mahwāt (f)	مهواة
trench (e.g. Mariana ~)	xandaq (m)	خندق

| current (Ocean ~) | tayyār (m) | تيّار |
| to surround (bathe) | aḥāṭ | أحاط |

shore	sāḥil (m)	ساحل
coast	sāḥil (m)	ساحل
flow (flood tide)	madd (m)	مدّ
ebb (ebb tide)	ʒazr (m)	جزر
shoal	miyāh ḍaḥla (f)	مياه ضحلة
bottom (~ of the sea)	qāʿ (m)	قاع
wave	mawʒa (f)	موجة
crest (~ of a wave)	qimmat mawʒa (f)	قمّة موجة
spume (sea foam)	zabad al baḥr (m)	زبد البحر
storm (sea storm)	ʿāṣifa (f)	عاصفة
hurricane	iʿṣār (m)	إعصار
tsunami	tsunāmi (m)	تسونامي
calm (dead ~)	hudūʾ (m)	هدوء
quiet, calm (adj)	hādiʾ	هادئ
pole	quṭb (m)	قطب
polar (adj)	quṭby	قطبيّ
latitude	ʿarḍ (m)	عرض
longitude	ṭūl (m)	طول
parallel	mutawāzi (m)	متواز
equator	χaṭṭ al istiwāʾ (m)	خط الإستواء
sky	samāʾ (f)	سماء
horizon	ufuq (m)	أفق
air	hawāʾ (m)	هواء
lighthouse	manāra (f)	منارة
to dive (vi)	ɣāṣ	غاص
to sink (ab. boat)	ɣariq	غرق
treasure	kunūz (pl)	كنوز

78. Seas & Oceans names

Atlantic Ocean	al muḥīṭ al aṭlasiy (m)	المحيط الأطلسيّ
Indian Ocean	al muḥīṭ al hindiy (m)	المحيط الهنديّ
Pacific Ocean	al muḥīṭ al hādiʾ (m)	المحيط الهادئ
Arctic Ocean	al muḥīṭ il mutaʒammid aʃ ʃimāliy (m)	المحيط المتجمّد الشماليّ
Black Sea	al baḥr al aswad (m)	البحر الأسود
Red Sea	al baḥr al aḥmar (m)	البحر الأحمر
Yellow Sea	al baḥr al aṣfar (m)	البحر الأصفر
White Sea	al baḥr al abyaḍ (m)	البحر الأبيض
Caspian Sea	baḥr qazwīn (m)	بحر قزوين
Dead Sea	al baḥr al mayyit (m)	البحر الميّت
Mediterranean Sea	al baḥr al abyaḍ al mutawassiṭ (m)	البحر الأبيض المتوسّط
Aegean Sea	baḥr ʾiʒah (m)	بحر إيجة
Adriatic Sea	al baḥr al adriyatīkiy (m)	البحر الأدرياتيكيّ

Arabian Sea	bahr al 'arab (m)	بحر العرب
Sea of Japan	bahr al yabān (m)	بحر اليابان
Bering Sea	bahr birinʒ (m)	بحر بيرينغ
South China Sea	bahr aṣ ṣīn al ʒanūbiy (m)	بحر الصين الجنويّ

Coral Sea	bahr al marʒān (m)	بحر المرجان
Tasman Sea	bahr tasmān (m)	بحر تسمان
Caribbean Sea	al bahr al karībiy (m)	البحر الكاريبيّ

| Barents Sea | bahr barints (m) | بحر بارينس |
| Kara Sea | bahr kara (m) | بحر كارا |

North Sea	bahr aʃ ʃimāl (m)	بحر الشمال
Baltic Sea	al bahr al balṭīq (m)	البحر البلطيق
Norwegian Sea	bahr an narwīʒ (m)	بحر النرويج

79. Mountains

mountain	ʒabal (m)	جبل
mountain range	silsilat ʒibāl (f)	سلسلة جبال
mountain ridge	qimam ʒabaliyya (pl)	قمم جبليّة

summit, top	qimma (f)	قمّة
peak	qimma (f)	قمّة
foot (~ of the mountain)	asfal (m)	أسفل
slope (mountainside)	munhadar (m)	منحدر

volcano	burkān (m)	بركان
active volcano	burkān naʃiṭ (m)	بركان نشط
dormant volcano	burkān xāmid (m)	بركان خامد

eruption	θawrān (m)	ثوران
crater	fūhat al burkān (f)	فوهة البركان
magma	māɣma (f)	ماغما
lava	humam burkāniyya (pl)	حمم بركانيّة
molten (~ lava)	munṣahira	منصهرة

canyon	tal'a (m)	تلعة
gorge	wādi ḍayyiq (m)	واد ضيّق
crevice	ʃaqq (m)	شقّ
abyss (chasm)	hāwiya (f)	هاوية

pass, col	mamarr ʒabaliy (m)	ممرّ جبليّ
plateau	haḍba (f)	هضبة
cliff	ʒurf (m)	جرف
hill	tall (m)	تلّ

glacier	nahr ʒalīdiy (m)	نهر جليديّ
waterfall	ʃallāl (m)	شلّال
geyser	fawwāra hārra (f)	فوّارة حارّة
lake	buhayra (f)	بحيرة

| plain | sahl (m) | سهل |
| landscape | manẓar ṭabīʿiy (m) | منظر طبيعيّ |

echo	ṣada (m)	صدى
alpinist	mutasalliq al ʒibāl (m)	متسلق الجبال
rock climber	mutasalliq ṣuxūr (m)	متسلق صخور
to conquer (in climbing)	taɣallab 'ala	تغلب على
climb (an easy ~)	tasalluq (m)	تسلق

80. Mountains names

The Alps	ʒibāl al alb (pl)	جبال الألب
Mont Blanc	mūn blūn (m)	مون بلون
The Pyrenees	ʒibāl al barānis (pl)	جبال البرانس
The Carpathians	ʒibāl al karbāt (pl)	جبال الكاربيات
The Ural Mountains	ʒibāl al 'ūrāl (pl)	جبال الأورال
The Caucasus Mountains	ʒibāl al qawqāz (pl)	جبال القوقاز
Mount Elbrus	ʒabal ilbrūs (m)	جبل إلبروس
The Altai Mountains	ʒibāl altāy (pl)	جبال ألتاي
The Tian Shan	ʒibāl tian ʃan (pl)	جبال تيان شان
The Pamirs	ʒibāl bamīr (pl)	جبال بامير
The Himalayas	himalāya (pl)	هيمالايا
Mount Everest	ʒabal ivirist (m)	جبل افرست
The Andes	ʒibāl al andīz (pl)	جبال الأنديز
Mount Kilimanjaro	ʒabal kilimanʒāru (m)	جبل كليمنجارو

81. Rivers

river	nahr (m)	نهر
spring (natural source)	'ayn (m)	عين
riverbed (river channel)	maʒra an nahr (m)	مجرى النهر
basin (river valley)	ḥawḍ (m)	حوض
to flow into ...	ṣabb fi ...	صبّ في...
tributary	rāfid (m)	رافد
bank (river ~)	ḍiffa (f)	ضفة
current (stream)	tayyār (m)	تيّار
downstream (adv)	f ittiʒāh maʒra an nahr	في إتجاه مجرى النهر
upstream (adv)	ḍidd at tayyār	ضد التيّار
inundation	ɣamr (m)	غمر
flooding	fayaḍān (m)	فيضان
to overflow (vi)	fāḍ	فاض
to flood (vt)	ɣamar	غمر
shallow (shoal)	miyāh ḍaḥla (f)	مياه ضحلة
rapids	munḥadar an nahr (m)	منحدر النهر
dam	sadd (m)	سدّ
canal	qanāt (f)	قناة
reservoir (artificial lake)	xazzān mā'iy (m)	خزّان مائيّ

sluice, lock	hawīs (m)	هويس
water body (pond, etc.)	maṣṭaḥ māʾiy (m)	مسطح مائيّ
swamp (marshland)	mustanqaʿ (m)	مستنقع
bog, marsh	mustanqaʿ (m)	مستنقع
whirlpool	dawwāma (f)	دوّامة
stream (brook)	ʒadwal māʾiy (m)	جدول مائيّ
drinking (ab. water)	aʃ ʃurb	الشرب
fresh (~ water)	ʿaðb	عذب
ice	ʒalīd (m)	جليد
to freeze over (ab. river, etc.)	taʒammad	تجمّد

82. Rivers names

Seine	nahr as sīn (m)	نهر السين
Loire	nahr al lua:r (m)	نهر اللوار
Thames	nahr at tīmz (m)	نهر التيمز
Rhine	nahr ar rayn (m)	نهر الراين
Danube	nahr ad danūb (m)	نهر الدانوب
Volga	nahr al vulɣa (m)	نهر الفولغا
Don	nahr ad dūn (m)	نهر الدون
Lena	nahr līna (m)	نهر لينا
Yellow River	an nahr al aṣfar (m)	النهر الأصفر
Yangtze	nahr al yanɣtsi (m)	نهر اليانغتسي
Mekong	nahr al mikunɣ (m)	نهر الميكونغ
Ganges	nahr al ɣānʒ (m)	نهر الغانج
Nile River	nahr an nīl (m)	نهر النيل
Congo River	nahr al kunɣu (m)	نهر الكنغو
Okavango River	nahr ukavanʒu (m)	نهر اوكافانجو
Zambezi River	nahr az zambizi (m)	نهر الزمبيزي
Limpopo River	nahr limbubu (m)	نهر ليمبوبو
Mississippi River	nahr al mississibbi (m)	نهر الميسيسيبي

83. Forest

forest, wood	ɣāba (f)	غابة
forest (as adj)	ɣāba	غابة
thick forest	ɣāba kaθīfa (f)	غابة كثيفة
grove	ɣāba ṣaɣīra (f)	غابة صغيرة
forest clearing	minṭaqa uzīlat minha al aʃʒār (f)	منطقة أزيلت منها الأشجار
thicket	aʒama (f)	أجمة
scrubland	ʃuʒayrāt (pl)	شجيرات
footpath (troddenpath)	mamarr (m)	ممرّ
gully	wādi ḍayyiq (m)	واد ضيّق

tree	ʃaʒara (f)	شجرة
leaf	waraqa (f)	ورقة
leaves (foliage)	waraq (m)	ورق
fall of leaves	tasāquṭ al awrāq (m)	تساقط الأوراق
to fall (ab. leaves)	saqaṭ	سقط
top (of the tree)	ra's (m)	رأس
branch	ɣuṣn (m)	غصن
bough	ɣuṣn (m)	غصن
bud (on shrub, tree)	burʿum (m)	برعم
needle (of the pine tree)	ʃawka (f)	شوكة
fir cone	kūz aṣ ṣanawbar (m)	كوز الصنوبر
tree hollow	ʒawf (m)	جوف
nest	ʿuʃʃ (m)	عش
burrow (animal hole)	ʒuḥr (m)	جحر
trunk	ʒiðʿ (m)	جذع
root	ʒiðr (m)	جذر
bark	liḥāʾ (m)	لحاء
moss	ṭuḥlub (m)	طحلب
to uproot (remove trees or tree stumps)	iqtalaʿ	إقتلع
to chop down	qaṭaʿ	قطع
to deforest (vt)	azāl al ɣābāt	أزال الغابات
tree stump	ʒiðʿ aʃ ʃaʒara (m)	جذع الشجرة
campfire	nār muxayyam (m)	نار مخيّم
forest fire	ḥarīq ɣāba (m)	حريق غابة
to extinguish (vt)	aṭfaʾ	أطفأ
forest ranger	ḥāris al ɣāba (m)	حارس الغابة
protection	ḥimāya (f)	حماية
to protect (~ nature)	ḥama	حمى
poacher	sāriq aṣ ṣayd (m)	سارق الصيد
steel trap	maṣyada (f)	مصيدة
to gather, to pick (vt)	ʒamaʿ	جمع
to lose one's way	tāh	تاه

84. Natural resources

natural resources	θarawāt ṭabīʿiyya (pl)	ثروات طبيعيّة
minerals	maʿādin (pl)	معادن
deposits	makāmin (pl)	مكامن
field (e.g. oilfield)	ḥaql (m)	حقل
to mine (extract)	istaxraʒ	إستخرج
mining (extraction)	istixrāʒ (m)	إستخراج
ore	xām (m)	خام
mine (e.g. for coal)	manʒam (m)	منجم
shaft (mine ~)	manʒam (m)	منجم

miner	'āmil manʒam (m)	عامل منجم
gas (natural ~)	ɣāz (m)	غاز
gas pipeline	χaṭṭ anābīb ɣāz (m)	خط أنابيب غاز

oil (petroleum)	naft (m)	نفط
oil pipeline	anābīb an naft (pl)	أنابيب النفط
oil well	bi'r an naft (m)	بئر النفط
derrick (tower)	ḥaffāra (f)	حفّارة
tanker	nāqilat an naft (f)	ناقلة النفط

sand	raml (m)	رمل
limestone	ḥaʒar kalsiy (m)	حجر كلسيّ
gravel	ḥaṣa (m)	حصى
peat	χaθθ faḥm nabātiy (m)	خثّ فحم نباتيّ
clay	ṭīn (m)	طين
coal	faḥm (m)	فحم

iron (ore)	ḥadīd (m)	حديد
gold	ðahab (m)	ذهب
silver	fiḍḍa (f)	فضّة
nickel	nikil (m)	نيكل
copper	nuḥās (m)	نحاس

zinc	zink (m)	زنك
manganese	manɣanīz (m)	منغنيز
mercury	zi'baq (m)	زئبق
lead	ruṣāṣ (m)	رصاص

mineral	ma'dan (m)	معدن
crystal	ballūra (f)	بلّورة
marble	ruχām (m)	رخام
uranium	yurānuim (m)	يورانيوم

85. Weather

weather	ṭaqs (m)	طقس
weather forecast	naʃra ʒawwiyya (f)	نشرة جوّية
temperature	ḥarāra (f)	حرارة
thermometer	tirmūmitr (m)	ترمومتر
barometer	barūmitr (m)	بارومتر

humid (adj)	raṭib	رطب
humidity	ruṭūba (f)	رطوبة
heat (extreme ~)	ḥarāra (f)	حرارة
hot (torrid)	ḥārr	حارّ
it's hot	al ʒaww ḥārr	الجوّ حارّ

| it's warm | al ʒaww dāfi' | الجوّ دافئ |
| warm (moderately hot) | dāfi' | دافئ |

it's cold	al ʒaww bārid	الجوّ بارد
cold (adj)	bārid	بارد
sun	ʃams (f)	شمس
to shine (vi)	aḍā'	أضاء

sunny (day)	muʃmis	مشمس
to come up (vi)	ʃaraq	شرق
to set (vi)	ɣarab	غرب

cloud	saħāba (f)	سحابة
cloudy (adj)	ɣā'im	غائم
rain cloud	saħābat maṭar (f)	سحابة مطر
somber (gloomy)	ɣā'im	غائم

rain	maṭar (m)	مطر
it's raining	innaha tamṭur	إنّها تمطر
rainy (~ day, weather)	mumṭir	ممطر
to drizzle (vi)	raðð	رذّ

pouring rain	maṭar munhamir (f)	مطر منهمر
downpour	maṭar ɣazīr (m)	مطر غزير
heavy (e.g. ~ rain)	ʃadīd	شديد
puddle	birka (f)	بركة
to get wet (in rain)	ibtall	إبتلّ

fog (mist)	ḍabāb (m)	ضباب
foggy	muḍabbab	مضبّب
snow	θalʒ (m)	ثلج
it's snowing	innaha taθluʒ	إنّها تثلج

86. Severe weather. Natural disasters

thunderstorm	'āṣifa ra'diyya (f)	عاصفة رعديّة
lightning (~ strike)	barq (m)	برق
to flash (vi)	baraq	برق

thunder	ra'd (m)	رعد
to thunder (vi)	ra'ad	رعد
it's thundering	tar'ad as samā'	ترعد السماء

| hail | maṭar bard (m) | مطر برد |
| it's hailing | tamṭur as samā' bardan | تمطر السماء بردًا |

| to flood (vt) | ɣamar | غمر |
| flood, inundation | fayaḍān (m) | فيضان |

earthquake	zilzāl (m)	زلزال
tremor, shoke	hazza arḍiyya (f)	هزّة أرضيّة
epicentre	markaz az zilzāl (m)	مركز الزلزال

| eruption | θawrān (m) | ثوران |
| lava | ħumam burkāniyya (pl) | حمم بركانيّة |

| twister, tornado | i'ṣār (m) | إعصار |
| typhoon | ṭūfān (m) | طوفان |

hurricane	i'ṣār (m)	إعصار
storm	'āṣifa (f)	عاصفة
tsunami	tsunāmi (m)	تسونامي

cyclone	iʻṣār (m)	إعصار
bad weather	ṭaqs sayyiʼ (m)	طقس سيّء
fire (accident)	ḥarīq (m)	حريق
disaster	kāriθa (f)	كارثة
meteorite	haʒar nayzakiy (m)	حجر نيزكيّ
avalanche	inhiyār θalʒiy (m)	إنهيار ثلجيّ
snowslide	inhiyār θalʒiy (m)	إنهيار ثلجيّ
blizzard	ʻāṣifa θalʒiyya (f)	عاصفة ثلجيّة
snowstorm	ʻāṣifa θalʒiyya (f)	عاصفة ثلجيّة

FAUNA

87. Mammals. Predators

predator	ḥayawān muftaris (m)	حيوان مفترس
tiger	namir (m)	نمر
lion	asad (m)	أسد
wolf	ði'b (m)	ذئب
fox	θaʻlab (m)	ثعلب
jaguar	namir amrīkiy (m)	نمر أمريكيّ
leopard	fahd (m)	فهد
cheetah	namir ṣayyād (m)	نمر صيّاد
black panther	namir aswad (m)	نمر أسود
puma	būma (m)	بوما
snow leopard	namir aθ θulūʒ (m)	نمر الثلوج
lynx	waʃaq (m)	وشق
coyote	qayūṭ (m)	قيوط
jackal	ibn 'āwa (m)	ابن آوى
hyena	ḍabuʻ (m)	ضبع

88. Wild animals

animal	ḥayawān (m)	حيوان
beast (animal)	ḥayawān (m)	حيوان
squirrel	sinʒāb (m)	سنجاب
hedgehog	qumfuð (m)	قنفذ
hare	arnab barriy (m)	أرنب برّيّ
rabbit	arnab (m)	أرنب
badger	ɣarīr (m)	غرير
raccoon	rākūn (m)	راكون
hamster	qidād (m)	قداد
marmot	marmuṭ (m)	مرموط
mole	χuld (m)	خلد
mouse	fa'r (m)	فأر
rat	ʒurað (m)	جرذ
bat	χuffāʃ (m)	خفّاش
ermine	qāqum (m)	قاقم
sable	sammūr (m)	سمّور
marten	dalaq (m)	دلق
weasel	ibn ʻirs (m)	إبن عرس
mink	mink (m)	منك

| beaver | qundus (m) | قندس |
| otter | quḍā'a (f) | قضاعة |

horse	ḥiṣān (m)	حصان
moose	mūz (m)	موظ
deer	ayyil (m)	أَيِل
camel	ʒamal (m)	جمل

bison	bisūn (m)	بيسون
wisent	θawr barriy (m)	ثور بَرِّيَ
buffalo	ʒāmūs (m)	جاموس

zebra	ḥimār zarad (m)	حمار زرد
antelope	ẓabiy (m)	ظبي
roe deer	yaḥmūr (m)	يحمور
fallow deer	ayyil asmar urubbiy (m)	أَيِل أسمر أوروبيَ
chamois	ʃamwāh (f)	شامواه
wild boar	χinzīr barriy (m)	خنزير بَرِّيَ

whale	ḥūt (m)	حوت
seal	fuqma (f)	فقمة
walrus	faẓẓ (m)	فظّ
fur seal	fuqmat al firā' (f)	فقمة الفراء
dolphin	dilfīn (m)	دلفين

bear	dubb (m)	دبّ
polar bear	dubb quṭbiy (m)	دبّ قطبيَ
panda	bānda (m)	باندا

monkey	qird (m)	قرد
chimpanzee	ʃimbanzi (m)	شيمبانزي
orangutan	urangutān (m)	أورنغوتان
gorilla	ɣurīlla (f)	غوريلا
macaque	qird al makāk (m)	قرد المكاك
gibbon	ʒibbūn (m)	جيبون

elephant	fīl (m)	فيل
rhinoceros	χartīt (m)	خرتيت
giraffe	zarāfa (f)	زرافة
hippopotamus	faras an nahr (m)	فرس النهر

| kangaroo | kanɣar (m) | كنغر |
| koala (bear) | kuala (m) | كوالا |

mongoose	nims (m)	نمس
chinchilla	ʃinʃila (f)	شنشيلة
skunk	ẓaribān (m)	ظربان
porcupine	nīṣ (m)	نيص

89. Domestic animals

cat	qiṭṭa (f)	قطّة
tomcat	ðakar al qiṭṭ (m)	ذكر القطّ
dog	kalb (m)	كلب

horse	ḥiṣān (m)	حصان
stallion (male horse)	faḥl al xayl (m)	فحل الخيل
mare	unθa al faras (f)	أنثى الفرس
cow	baqara (f)	بقرة
bull	θawr (m)	ثور
ox	θawr (m)	ثور
sheep (ewe)	xarūf (f)	خروف
ram	kabʃ (m)	كبش
goat	māʿiz (m)	ماعز
billy goat, he-goat	ðakar al māʿið (m)	ذكر الماعز
donkey	ḥimār (m)	حمار
mule	bayl (m)	بغل
pig	xinzīr (m)	خنزير
piglet	xannūṣ (m)	خنّوص
rabbit	arnab (m)	أرنب
hen (chicken)	daʒāʒa (f)	دجاجة
cock	dīk (m)	ديك
duck	baṭṭa (f)	بطّة
drake	ðakar al baṭṭ (m)	ذكر البطّ
goose	iwazza (f)	إوزّة
tom turkey, gobbler	dīk rūmiy (m)	ديك روميّ
turkey (hen)	daʒāʒ rūmiy (m)	دجاج روميّ
domestic animals	ḥayawānāt dawāʒin (pl)	حيوانات دواجن
tame (e.g. ~ hamster)	alīf	أليف
to tame (vt)	allaf	ألّف
to breed (vt)	rabba	ربّى
farm	mazraʿa (f)	مزرعة
poultry	ṭuyūr dāʒina (pl)	طيور داجنة
cattle	māʃiya (f)	ماشية
herd (cattle)	qaṭīʿ (m)	قطيع
stable	isṭabl xayl (m)	إسطبل خيل
pigsty	ḥazīrat al xanāzīr (f)	حظيرة الخنازير
cowshed	zirībat al baqar (f)	زريبة البقر
rabbit hutch	qunn al arānib (m)	قنّ الأرانب
hen house	qunn ad daʒāʒ (m)	قنّ الدجاج

90. Birds

bird	ṭāʾir (m)	طائر
pigeon	ḥamāma (f)	حمامة
sparrow	ʿuṣfūr (m)	عصفور
tit (great tit)	qurquf (m)	قرقف
magpie	ʿaqʿaq (m)	عقعق
raven	yurāb aswad (m)	غراب أسود

crow	ɣurāb (m)	غراب
jackdaw	zāɣ (m)	زاغ
rook	ɣurāb al qayẓ (m)	غراب القيظ

duck	baṭṭa (f)	بطة
goose	iwazza (f)	إوزة
pheasant	tadarruʒ (m)	تدرج

eagle	nasr (m)	نسر
hawk	bāz (m)	باز
falcon	ṣaqr (m)	صقر
vulture	raχam (m)	رخم
condor (Andean ~)	kundūr (m)	كندور

swan	timma (m)	تمّة
crane	kurkiy (m)	كركي
stork	laqlaq (m)	لقلق

parrot	babaɣā' (m)	ببغاء
hummingbird	ṭannān (m)	طنّان
peacock	ṭāwūs (m)	طاووس

ostrich	na'āma (f)	نعامة
heron	balaʃūn (m)	بلشون
flamingo	nuḥām wardiy (m)	نحام ورديّ
pelican	baʒa'a (f)	بجعة

| nightingale | bulbul (m) | بلبل |
| swallow | sunūnū (m) | سنونو |

thrush	sumna (m)	سمنة
song thrush	summuna muɣarrida (m)	سمنة مغرّدة
blackbird	ʃaḥrūr aswad (m)	شحرور أسود

swift	samāma (m)	سمامة
lark	qubbara (f)	قبّرة
quail	sammān (m)	سمّان

woodpecker	naqqār al χaʃab (m)	نقّار الخشب
cuckoo	waqwāq (m)	وقواق
owl	būma (f)	بومة
eagle owl	būm urāsiy (m)	بوم أوراسيّ
wood grouse	dīk il χalanʒ (m)	ديك الخلنج
black grouse	ṭayhūʒ aswad (m)	طيهوج أسود
partridge	ḥaʒal (m)	حجل

starling	zurzūr (m)	زرزور
canary	kanāriy (m)	كناريّ
hazel grouse	ṭayhūʒ il bunduq (m)	طيهوج البندق

| chaffinch | ʃurʃūr (m) | شرشور |
| bullfinch | diɣnāʃ (m) | دغناش |

seagull	nawras (m)	نورس
albatross	al qaṭras (m)	القطرس
penguin	biṭrīq (m)	بطريق

91. Fish. Marine animals

bream	abramīs (m)	أبراميس
carp	ʃabbūṭ (m)	شبّوط
perch	farχ (m)	فرخ
catfish	qarmūṭ (m)	قرموط
pike	samak al karāki (m)	سمك الكراكي

| salmon | salmūn (m) | سلمون |
| sturgeon | ḥaʃʃ (m) | حفش |

herring	rinʒa (f)	رنجة
Atlantic salmon	salmūn aṭlasiy (m)	سلمون أطلسيّ
mackerel	usqumriy (m)	أسقمريّ
flatfish	samak mufalṭaḥ (f)	سمك مفلطح

zander, pike perch	samak sandar (m)	سمك سندر
cod	qudd (m)	قدّ
tuna	tūna (f)	تونة
trout	salmūn muraqqaṭ (m)	سلمون مرقّط

eel	ḥankalīs (m)	حنكليس
electric ray	ra''ād (m)	رعّاد
moray eel	murāy (m)	موراي
piranha	birāna (f)	بيرانا

shark	qirʃ (m)	قرش
dolphin	dilfīn (m)	دلفين
whale	ḥūt (m)	حوت

crab	salṭa'ūn (m)	سلطعون
jellyfish	qindīl al baḥr (m)	قنديل البحر
octopus	uχṭubūṭ (m)	أخطبوط

starfish	naʒmat al baḥr (f)	نجمة البحر
sea urchin	qumfuð al baḥr (m)	قنفذ البحر
seahorse	ḥiṣān al baḥr (m)	فرس البحر

oyster	maḥār (m)	محار
prawn	ʒambari (m)	جمبريّ
lobster	istakūza (f)	إستكوزا
spiny lobster	karkand ʃāik (m)	كركند شائك

92. Amphibians. Reptiles

| snake | θu'bān (m) | ثعبان |
| venomous (snake) | sāmm | سامّ |

viper	af'a (f)	أفعى
cobra	kūbra (m)	كوبرا
python	biθūn (m)	بيثون
boa	buwā' (f)	بواء
grass snake	θu'bān al 'uʃb (m)	ثعبان العشب

rattle snake	afʿa al ʒalʒala (f)	أفعى الجلجلة
anaconda	anakūnda (f)	أناكوندا
lizard	siḥliyya (f)	سحليّة
iguana	iɣwāna (f)	إغوانة
monitor lizard	waral (m)	ورل
salamander	samandar (m)	سمندر
chameleon	ḥirbā' (f)	حرباء
scorpion	ʿaqrab (m)	عقرب
turtle	sulaḥfāt (f)	سلحفاة
frog	ḍifḍaʿ (m)	ضفدع
toad	ḍifḍaʿ aṭ ṭīn (m)	ضفدع الطين
crocodile	timsāḥ (m)	تمساح

93. Insects

insect	ḥaʃara (f)	حشرة
butterfly	farāʃa (f)	فراشة
ant	namla (f)	نملة
fly	ðubāba (f)	ذبابة
mosquito	namūsa (f)	ناموسة
beetle	χunfusa (f)	خنفسة
wasp	dabbūr (m)	دبّور
bee	naḥla (f)	نحلة
bumblebee	naḥla ṭannāna (f)	نحلة طنّانة
gadfly (botfly)	naʿra (f)	نعرة
spider	ʿankabūt (m)	عنكبوت
spider's web	nasīʒ ʿankabūt (m)	نسيج عنكبوت
dragonfly	yaʿsūb (m)	يعسوب
grasshopper	ʒarād (m)	جراد
moth (night butterfly)	ʿitta (f)	عتّة
cockroach	ṣurṣūr (m)	صرصور
tick	qurāda (f)	قرادة
flea	burɣūθ (m)	برغوث
midge	baʿūḍa (f)	بعوضة
locust	ʒarād (m)	جراد
snail	ḥalzūn (m)	حلزون
cricket	ṣarrār al layl (m)	صرّار الليل
firefly	yarāʿa muḍīʿa (f)	يراعة مضيئة
ladybird	daʿsūqa (f)	دعسوقة
cockchafer	χunfusa kabīra (f)	خنفسة كبيرة
leech	ʿalaqa (f)	علقة
caterpillar	yasrūʿ (m)	يسروع
earthworm	dūda (f)	دودة
larva	yaraqa (f)	يرقة

FLORA

94. Trees

tree	ʃaʒara (f)	شجرة
deciduous (adj)	nafḍiyya	نفضيّة
coniferous (adj)	ṣanawbariyya	صنوبريّة
evergreen (adj)	dā'imat al xuḍra	دائمة الخضرة
apple tree	ʃaʒarat tuffāḥ (f)	شجرة تفّاح
pear tree	ʃaʒarat kummaθra (f)	شجرة كمّثرى
cherry tree	ʃaʒarat karaz (f)	شجرة كرز
plum tree	ʃaʒarat barqūq (f)	شجرة برقوق
birch	batūla (f)	بتولا
oak	ballūṭ (f)	بلّوط
linden tree	ʃaʒarat zayzafūn (f)	شجرة زيزفون
aspen	ḥawr raʒrāʒ (m)	حور رجراج
maple	qayqab (f)	قيقب
spruce	ratinaʒ (f)	راتينج
pine	ṣanawbar (f)	صنوبر
larch	arziyya (f)	أرزيّة
fir tree	tannūb (f)	تنّوب
cedar	arz (f)	أرز
poplar	ḥawr (f)	حور
rowan	ɣubayrā' (f)	غبيراء
willow	ṣafṣāf (f)	صفصاف
alder	ʒār il mā' (m)	جار الماء
beech	zān (m)	زان
elm	dardār (f)	دردار
ash (tree)	marān (f)	مران
chestnut	kastanā' (f)	كستناء
magnolia	maɣnūliya (f)	مغنوليا
palm tree	naxla (f)	نخلة
cypress	sarw (f)	سرو
mangrove	ayka sāḥiliyya (f)	أيكة ساحليّة
baobab	bāubāb (f)	باوباب
eucalyptus	ukaliptus (f)	أوكاليبتوس
sequoia	siqūya (f)	سيكويا

95. Shrubs

bush	ʃuʒayra (f)	شجيرة
shrub	ʃuʒayrāt (pl)	شجيرات

| grapevine | karma (f) | كرمة |
| vineyard | karam (m) | كرم |

raspberry bush	tūt al 'ullayq al aḥmar (m)	توت العليق الأحمر
redcurrant bush	kiʃmiʃ aḥmar (m)	كشمش أحمر
gooseberry bush	'inab aθ θa'lab (m)	عنب الثعلب

acacia	sanṭ (f)	سنط
barberry	amīr barīs (m)	أمير باريس
jasmine	yāsmīn (m)	ياسمين

juniper	'ar'ar (m)	عرعر
rosebush	ʃuʒayrat ward (f)	شجيرة ورد
dog rose	ward ʒabaliy (m)	ورد جبليّ

96. Fruits. Berries

fruit	θamra (f)	ثمرة
fruits	θamr (m)	ثمر
apple	tuffāḥa (f)	تفّاحة

| pear | kummaθra (f) | كمّثرى |
| plum | barqūq (m) | برقوق |

strawberry (garden ~)	farawla (f)	فراولة
cherry	karaz (m)	كرز
grape	'inab (m)	عنب

raspberry	tūt al 'ullayq al aḥmar (m)	توت العليق الأحمر
blackcurrant	'inab aθ θa'lab al aswad (m)	عنب الثعلب الأسود
redcurrant	kiʃmiʃ aḥmar (m)	كشمش أحمر

| gooseberry | 'inab aθ θa'lab (m) | عنب الثعلب |
| cranberry | tūt aḥmar barriy (m) | توت أحمر برّيّ |

orange	burtuqāl (m)	برتقال
tangerine	yūsufiy (m)	يوسفي
pineapple	ananās (m)	أناناس

| banana | mawz (m) | موز |
| date | tamr (m) | تمر |

lemon	laymūn (m)	ليمون
apricot	miʃmiʃ (f)	مشمش
peach	durrāq (m)	دراق

| kiwi | kiwi (m) | كيوي |
| grapefruit | zinbā' (m) | زنباع |

berry	ḥabba (f)	حبّة
berries	ḥabbāt (pl)	حبّات
cowberry	'inab aθ θawr (m)	عنب الثور
wild strawberry	farāwla barriyya (f)	فراولة برّية
bilberry	'inab al aḥrāʒ (m)	عنب الأحراج

97. Flowers. Plants

flower	zahra (f)	زهرة
bouquet (of flowers)	bāqat zuhūr (f)	باقة زهور
rose (flower)	warda (f)	وردة
tulip	tulīb (f)	توليب
carnation	qurumful (m)	قرنفل
gladiolus	dalbūθ (f)	دلبوث
cornflower	turunʃāh (m)	ترنشاه
harebell	ʒarīs (m)	جريس
dandelion	hindibā' (f)	هندباء
camomile	babunʒ (m)	بابونج
aloe	aluwwa (m)	أَلوَة
cactus	ṣabbār (m)	صبّار
rubber plant, ficus	tīn (m)	تين
lily	sawsan (m)	سوسن
geranium	ibrat ar rā'i (f)	إبرة الراعي
hyacinth	zanbaq (f)	زنبق
mimosa	mimūza (f)	ميموزا
narcissus	narʒis (f)	نرجس
nasturtium	abu χanʒar (f)	أبو خنجر
orchid	saḥlab (f)	سحلب
peony	fawniya (f)	فاوانيا
violet	banafsaʒ (f)	بنفسج
pansy	banafsaʒ muθallaθ (m)	بنفسج مثلث
forget-me-not	'āðān al fa'r (pl)	آذان الفأر
daisy	uqhuwān (f)	أقحوان
poppy	χaʃχāʃ (f)	خشخاش
hemp	qinnab (m)	قنب
mint	na'nā' (m)	نعناع
lily of the valley	sawsan al wādi (m)	سوسن الوادي
snowdrop	zahrat al laban (f)	زهرة اللبن
nettle	qarrāṣ (m)	قرّاص
sorrel	ḥammāḍ (m)	حمّاض
water lily	nilūfar (m)	نيلوفر
fern	saraχs (m)	سرخس
lichen	uʃna (f)	أشنة
conservatory (greenhouse)	daffa (f)	دفيئة
lawn	'uʃb (m)	عشب
flowerbed	ʒunaynat zuhūr (f)	جنينة زهور
plant	nabāt (m)	نبات
grass	'uʃb (m)	عشب
blade of grass	'uʃba (f)	عشبة

leaf	waraqa (f)	ورقة
petal	waraqat az zahra (f)	ورقة الزهرة
stem	sāq (f)	ساق
tuber	darnat nabāt (f)	درنة نبات

| young plant (shoot) | nabta saɣīra (f) | نبتة صغيرة |
| thorn | ʃawka (f) | شوكة |

to blossom (vi)	nawwar	نوّر
to fade, to wither	ðabal	ذبل
smell (odour)	rā'iḥa (f)	رائحة
to cut (flowers)	qaṭaʿ	قطع
to pick (a flower)	qaṭaf	قطف

98. Cereals, grains

grain	ḥubūb (pl)	حبوب
cereal crops	maḥāṣīl al ḥubūb (pl)	محاصيل الحبوب
ear (of barley, etc.)	sumbula (f)	سنبلة

wheat	qamḥ (m)	قمح
rye	ʒāwdār (m)	جاودار
oats	ʃūfān (m)	شوفان
millet	duxn (m)	دخن
barley	ʃaʿīr (m)	شعير

maize	ðura (f)	ذرة
rice	urz (m)	أرز
buckwheat	ḥinṭa sawdā' (f)	حنطة سوداء

pea plant	bisilla (f)	بسلة
kidney bean	faṣūliya (f)	فاصوليا
soya	fūl aṣ ṣūya (m)	فول الصويا
lentil	ʿadas (m)	عدس
beans (pulse crops)	fūl (m)	فول

COUNTRIES OF THE WORLD

99. Countries. Part 1

Afghanistan	afɣanistān (f)	أفغانستان
Albania	albāniya (f)	ألبانيا
Argentina	arʒantīn (f)	الأرجنتين
Armenia	armīniya (f)	أرمينيا
Australia	usturāliya (f)	أستراليا
Austria	an nimsa (f)	النمسا
Azerbaijan	aðarbiʒān (m)	أذربيجان

The Bahamas	ʒuzur bahāmas (pl)	جزر باهاماس
Bangladesh	banʒladīʃ (f)	بنجلاديش
Belarus	bilarūs (f)	بيلاروس
Belgium	balʒīka (f)	بلجيكا
Bolivia	bulīviya (f)	بوليفيا
Bosnia and Herzegovina	al busna wal hirsuk (f)	البوسنة والهرسك
Brazil	al brazīl (f)	البرازيل
Bulgaria	bulɣāriya (f)	بلغاريا

Cambodia	kambūdya (f)	كمبوديا
Canada	kanada (f)	كندا
Chile	tʃīli (f)	تشيلي
China	aş şīn (f)	الصين
Colombia	kulumbiya (f)	كولومبيا
Croatia	kruātiya (f)	كرواتيا
Cuba	kūba (f)	كوبا

| Cyprus | qubruş (f) | قبرص |
| Czech Republic | atʃ tʃīk (f) | التشيك |

Denmark	ad danimārk (f)	الدانمارك
Dominican Republic	ʒumhūriyyat ad duminikan (f)	جمهورية الدومينيكان
Ecuador	al iqwadūr (f)	الإكوادور
Egypt	mişr (f)	مصر
England	inʒiltirra (f)	إنجلترا
Estonia	istūniya (f)	إستونيا
Finland	finlanda (f)	فنلندا

| France | faransa (f) | فرنسا |
| French Polynesia | bulinīziya al faransiyya (f) | بولينيزيا الفرنسيّة |

Georgia	ʒūrʒiya (f)	جورجيا
Germany	almāniya (f)	ألمانيا
Ghana	ɣāna (f)	غانا
Great Britain	briṭāniya al 'uẓma (f)	بريطانيا العظمى
Greece	al yūnān (f)	اليونان
Haiti	haīti (f)	هايتي
Hungary	al maʒar (f)	المجر

100. Countries. Part 2

Iceland	'āyslanda (f)	آيسلندا
India	al hind (f)	الهند
Indonesia	indunīsiya (f)	إندونيسيا
Iran	'īrān (f)	إيران
Iraq	al 'irāq (m)	العراق
Ireland	irlanda (f)	أيرلندا
Israel	isrā'īl (f)	إسرائيل
Italy	iṭāliya (f)	إيطاليا

Jamaica	ʒamāyka (f)	جامايكا
Japan	al yabān (f)	اليابان
Jordan	al urdun (m)	الأردن
Kazakhstan	kazaχstān (f)	كازاخستان
Kenya	kiniya (f)	كينيا
Kirghizia	qirɣizistān (f)	قيرغيزستان
Kuwait	al kuwayt (f)	الكويت

Laos	lawus (f)	لاوس
Latvia	lātviya (f)	لاتفيا
Lebanon	lubnān (f)	لبنان
Libya	lībiya (f)	ليبيا
Liechtenstein	liʃtinʃtāyn (m)	ليشتنشتاين
Lithuania	litwāniya (f)	ليتوانيا
Luxembourg	luksimburɣ (f)	لوكسمبورغ

North Macedonia	maqdūniya (f)	مقدونيا
Madagascar	madaɣaʃqar (f)	مدغشقر
Malaysia	malīziya (f)	ماليزيا
Malta	malṭa (f)	مالطا
Mexico	al maksīk (f)	المكسيك

Moldova, Moldavia	muldāviya (f)	مولدافيا
Monaco	munāku (f)	موناكو
Mongolia	manɣūliya (f)	منغوليا
Montenegro	al ʒabal al aswad (m)	الجبل الأسود
Morocco	al maɣrib (m)	المغرب
Myanmar	myanmār (f)	ميانمار

Namibia	namībiya (f)	ناميبيا
Nepal	nibāl (f)	نيبال
Netherlands	hulanda (f)	هولندا
New Zealand	nyu zilanda (f)	نيوزيلندا
North Korea	kūria aʃ ʃimāliyya (f)	كوريا الشماليّة
Norway	an nirwīʒ (f)	النرويج

101. Countries. Part 3

Pakistan	bakistān (f)	باكستان
Palestine	filisṭīn (f)	فلسطين
Panama	banama (f)	بنما
Paraguay	baraɣwāy (f)	باراغواي

Peru	biru (f)	بيرو
Poland	bulanda (f)	بولندا
Portugal	al burtuɣāl (f)	البرتغال
Romania	rumāniya (f)	رومانيا
Russia	rūsiya (f)	روسيا
Saudi Arabia	as saʿūdiyya (f)	السعوديّة
Scotland	iskutlanda (f)	اسكتلندا
Senegal	as siniɣāl (f)	السنغال
Serbia	ṣirbiya (f)	صربيا
Slovakia	sluvākiya (f)	سلوفاكيا
Slovenia	sluvīniya (f)	سلوفينيا
South Africa	ʒumhūriyyat afrīqiya al ʒanūbiyya (f)	جمهريّة أفريقيا الجنوبيّة
South Korea	kuriya al ʒanūbiyya (f)	كوريا الجنوبيّة
Spain	isbāniya (f)	إسبانيا
Suriname	surinām (f)	سورينام
Sweden	as suwayd (f)	السويد
Switzerland	swīsra (f)	سويسرا
Syria	sūriya (f)	سوريا
Taiwan	taywān (f)	تايوان
Tajikistan	ṭaʒīkistān (f)	طاجيكستان
Tanzania	tanzāniya (f)	تنزانيا
Tasmania	tasmāniya (f)	تاسمانيا
Thailand	taylānd (f)	تايلاند
Tunisia	tūnis (f)	تونس
Turkey	turkiya (f)	تركيا
Turkmenistan	turkmānistān (f)	تركمانستان
Ukraine	ukrāniya (f)	أوكرانيا
United Arab Emirates	al imārāt al ʿarabiyya al muttaḥida (pl)	الإمارات العربيّة المتّحدة
United States of America	al wilāyāt al muttaḥida al amrīkiyya (pl)	الولايات المتّحدة الأمريكيّة
Uruguay	uruɣwāy (f)	الأوروغواي
Uzbekistan	uzbikistān (f)	أوزيكستان
Vatican City	al vatikān (m)	الفاتيكان
Venezuela	vinizwiyla (f)	فنزويلا
Vietnam	vitnām (f)	فيتنام
Zanzibar	zanʒibār (f)	زنجبار

www.ingramcontent.com/pod-product-compliance
Lightning Source LLC
Chambersburg PA
CBHW070832050426
42452CB00011B/2251

*9 7 8 1 7 8 7 1 6 7 1 8 6 *